YOU AND YOUR
AGING PARENTS

Discovery
House
PUBLISHERS

BOX 3566 · GRAND RAPIDS, MI 49501

*PUBLISHING BOOKS THAT FEED
THE SOUL WITH THE WORD OF GOD.*

YOU AND YOUR
AGING PARENTS

William L. Coleman

Discovery House Publishers is affiliated with Radio Bible Class,
Grand Rapids, Michigan 49501

Discovery House books are distributed to the trade by Thomas Nelson,
Publishers, Nashville, Tennessee 37214

Library of Congress Cataloging-in-Publication Data

Coleman, William L.
    You and your aging parents / William L. Coleman.
        p. cm.
    ISBN 0-929239-90-3
    1. Aging parents—United States. 2. Aging parents—Care—
United States. 3. Parent and adult child—United States. 4. Aging
parents—Care—Religious aspects—Christianity. I. Title.
HQ1063.6.C67   1994
306.874—dc20   94–31604
                                                                CIP

Printed in the United States of America

94 95 96 97 98 99 / CHG / 10 9 8 7 6 5 4 3 2 1

TABLE OF CONTENTS

Dedicated to

Helen Tingle Marshall

for providing me with a wonderful wife

With Appreciation

As is usually the case, there are too many people to thank. Groups at churches, camps, seminars and in living rooms have met with us and shared their stories. We are indebted to each and to all.

Nevertheless it is important to point out a few people who went the extra mile.

Bob DeVries and Carol Holquist of Discovery House have been excellent to work with, as anyone who knows them might guess. The project spread wings at a breakfast table nearly a year ago when they helped push it out of the nest.

Special appreciation is due to those who attended the Senior Adult Retreat at Covenant Cedars in Hordville, Nebraska. Those fun-loving campers told us what it was like to be aging but spirited parents.

Others sat in our home, ate chili, and told us about their experiences with helping their aging parents. They gave freely of themselves and were both outstanding resources and good friends.

Menno and Susanna Classen
Dale and Jean Jackson
Rich and Lois Janzen
Don and Joyce Kupfersmith
Val and Carol Oswald
Gary and Sandy Samuelson
Syd and Patty Widga

The stories and examples were collected from many people and places across the country. In most cases we have changed the accounts just enough to hide individual identities so they can keep the peace at their next family reunions.

THE SNOW-CAPPED MOUNTAINS

If you have driven in the beautiful Rocky Mountains, you know there is something new around each bend in the road. Trees, rocks, sheep, valleys, deer, rippling brooks, waterfalls, and new peaks are waiting as the happy traveler motors along.

Life is similar to that Colorado adventure. At our stage we have entered the snow-capped mountain region. The snow has begun to cover our parents' heads. And when we look in the mirror, most of us see flakes showing up on our own.

Every part of life has proved to be different. The area we are in now has new challenges quite unlike those of adolescence or young adulthood. Interacting with aging parents has its own peculiar set of peaks and valleys.

Older parents can be a blessing from God. Much depends on attitudes, preparation, and expectation. An eighty-three-year-old parent can enrich one's life in a deep spiritual and loving way. But this doesn't happen automatically. Each person involved needs to ask the Lord for special grace and understanding.

Expect this: Some days you will sit on the steps and laugh until you hurt because of something your parent said or did. Other days you'll shrug your shoulders and wonder what that phone call was about. And don't be surprised if on another occasion you become angry and frustrated over what happened last evening.

Parents are full of flavor. Sugar, salt, pepper, garlic, and cinnamon are just a few. They season our lives and, like most seasonings, they leave a wonderful taste one day and a bit of heartburn the next.

Since you bought this book and are taking the time to read it, I assume you are someone who cares. That's good. Caring attitudes and actions are close to the heart of God. Hopefully the book will furnish information and provide inspiration. Possibly it will even become a friend that you can sit down with and seek advice from periodically.

Age is a great thing. Maybe that's why God doesn't take us all young. Some things in life cannot be understood except through the eyes of experienced people who have been there.

Enjoy your relationship with elderly parents. God uses us to touch their lives and they to touch ours.

Bill Coleman
Aurora, Nebraska

1

ARE WE ADOPTING
OUR PARENTS?

Standing by the gate at the Lincoln Airport, neither my wife, Pat, nor I understood exactly how this was going to work. At any moment my aging father and stepmother would get off an airplane and begin their new life in Nebraska. We had no idea how they would affect our lives or how we would affect theirs.

Accompanied by my brother, Ed, my father rode in a wheelchair and my stepmother walked slowly through the door. We greeted each other like old army buddies, inquired about the trip, and headed for the baggage claim. Soon my brother was headed his own way back to Washington, D.C., and the rest of us drove toward our small town nearly seventy miles away.

My parents and I had gotten together no more than once every year or two for the past twenty years. While we weren't close, we got along well enough, and now they needed us. Instead of their going into a nursing home in D.C., we gave them the option of buying their own home and living in the tranquil atmosphere of the plains states.

We weren't sure of everything that went into the decision-making, but before long they came flying our way. We wanted them. We invited them. We were happy that they had made the choice to come. Now we were about to open a treasure chest and discover the benefits, blessings, surprises, and headaches of living with our aging parents.

You and Your Aging Parents

For the next four and a half years we touched each other's lives. Sometimes our experiences were warm and fuzzy; other times they were sharp and painful. Today they are both buried outside our little town among the farmers, pioneers, and war heroes of Hamilton County. When they were younger they never would have expected their headstones to be mounted here.

One way or another this story is similar to millions of others. In record numbers middle-age adults are becoming involved with their aging parents. Every day 5,000 new adults pass over that magic line and become sixty-five years old. There are thirty million such adults and the numbers will continue to gallop for at least the next ten years. Many of those who are sixty-five can be expected to live for another twenty or thirty years. An increasing number will top the century mark.

That's the good news. We are living longer and are generally in good health. But with these numbers comes a great deal of perplexity. How are middle-age children supposed to become involved with their aging parents? They have little or no training in the care, feeding, and entertaining of adult parents.

Suddenly they are flooded with gallons of questions they had never considered. Questions about housing, finances, health, relatives, exercise, and diets come pouring in. Quickly the adult child looks for instant answers but has trouble finding them. They need to find not only solutions, but solutions that everyone involved can accept.

Many times adult children long to become dictators. "You do this," "You live there," "Eat that," "Be ready at 6 o'clock," "Ask the doctor yourself." But peace comes only by struggle, and struggles take time, negotiation, understanding, and patience.

Don't be shocked if you are faced with these dilemmas:

• Your pensioned mother has just written a check for $2,000 to save the water buffaloes.

• Your seventy-year-old father starts dating a forty-five-year-old woman.

• Your mother is diagnosed with a heart disease and she refuses to return to the doctor.

• Your parents want to move into your upstairs bedroom.

• Your mother has moved in with a widower.

• Your father and mother are heading for a year in Siberia and want you to take care of their twin German shepherds.

• Your sister from Panama City calls and wants to know why you don't drop in to see the parents more often.

• The doctor says the family has to decide whether or not to use heroic measures.

Anyone who has been involved with aging parents can testify that these aren't unusual situations at all. Adult children become entangled in the process of helping other adults make major, deeply significant decisions.

We aren't alone

There are plenty of people who could share their experiences about dealing with aging parents. The National Institute on Aging says seventy percent of those in the fiftyish age group are living in the middle. That is, they have grandchildren of their own and also have one or two parents still living.

Since there are so many who fit into this situation, you should be able to find ways to network or connect experiences and share constructive approaches to helping. Often the best kind of help is to back off and let parents run their own show. But how do we know when to do that? Talking and listening to others in the same predicament gives us a wider view and allows us to see some options.

Few of us want to be the meddling adult child who interferes. If we don't have to parent our parents, it makes no sense to rush in and take over. But how are we to know if or when to step in?

The desire to lend a hand isn't as simple as it sounds. The real questions are:

- How much help is needed?
- How far can we afford to go?
- Where do their needs and our needs clash?
- How much energy do we have?
- Who is in charge here?
- Will we lose our identity if we help them?
- What strain will this place on our families?
- What happens to our travel and retirement plans?
- How will our grown children react?
- Should I give up my career?
- What if we never got along anyway?

Those are just a few starter questions. Each situation will produce its own challenges, bewilderment, and blessings.

Pick up your Bible

Aging parents are too complex and too important to take lightly. On day one, before the ball starts rolling, pick up your Bible and gain some spiritual insight. If the ball is already rolling, it's even more urgent that you turn to the Scriptures.

Frankly, some of us don't want to. We are afraid of the Bible. We are afraid that all it holds for us is one gigantic guilt trip. We are convinced that any reading will only dump limitless responsibility squarely on our shoulders.

On the contrary! The Bible leads us to an even-handed view of the problem. A careful reader will discover that we are discouraged from helping parents who can take care of themselves. We are admonished to lend a hand only when it's needed.

Let's begin by looking at a few Biblical directives. They are not listed here in any order of importance.

• *We want to help people in need.*

That's as basic as the Christian message itself. We can't afford to be selfish and look out only for ourselves.

"Each of you should look not only to your own interests, but also to the interests of others" (Philippians 2:4).

• *We need to take care of our family members.*

Relatives are priority. None of us can abandon family in order to meet the needs of strangers. Strangers and friends are important, and we respond to their problems. But we are forbidden to neglect our own in order to minister to others. First Timothy 5:8 is blunt and unequivocal.

"If anyone does not provide for his relatives, and especially for his immediate family, he has denied the faith and is worse than an unbeliever."

Some Pharisees refused to care for their parents. They insisted that they gave their goods to serve God and weren't obligated to provide for Mom and Dad (Mark 7:11). Jesus flatly condemned this attitude.

So far this is what many of us expected. But this isn't the entire picture. (The Bible discourages us from helping parents who are capable of helping themselves. If we don't learn this principle, we can become guilt-driven.)

• *Don't help parents who can help themselves.*

All things being equal—and things aren't always equal—parents should take care of their young children and children should not need to support their parents. The apostle Paul knew this was the normal way things should be handled.

Paul didn't want to be dependent on the Corinthian Christians even though he was their spiritual parent. "After all, children should not have to save up for their parents, but parents for their children" (2 Corinthians 12:14). To support his point he then used the accepted parent/child relationship.

But not all parents are able to provide for themselves in old age. Illness, calamity, bankruptcy, theft, job loss, and many other circumstances contribute to an inability to support oneself. In that situation Christians must do what they can. But if parents can care for themselves, they should. Read that sentence again.

Regularly I praise God that my parents brought their pension plans with them. As a struggling writer, I would have been hard-pressed to help them if they had not been financially independent. They put a down payment on a home and they cared for the property out of their resources. There was no doubt that they would do what they could, and we would help where they couldn't help themselves.

Never barge in and do what they can do for themselves.

• *We do harm by doing too much.*

The temptation is to step in and help too much too soon. Many good people, eager to give loving care, jump in far too quickly. Wise early Christians warned us against doing damage by helping perfectly able aging people. Churches wanted to help widows but they knew they could do as much harm as good. That led them to create rules governing how they would help. One regulation was that they refuse to help too soon.

In their case, if the widow was under sixty years of age the church said she could not be listed as a widow. She had too much living ahead to settle in and become dependent.

"No widow may be put on the list of widows unless she is over sixty, has been faithful to her husband . . ." (1 Timothy 5:9).

The principle is extremely practical. Don't let parents become dependent before their time. We could cut their active lives short by adopting them and supplying more care than they really need.

We have all heard great stories of people who have had their most rewarding years between sixty and eighty-five. None of us wants to steal these fruitful experiences.

2

NEVER STICK MOSES
IN THE ATTIC

You've probably heard the story about the Boy Scout who proudly reported to his mother.

"You should have seen us today. Three of us Boy Scouts helped an old lady cross the street."

"That's wonderful, son," she beamed, "but why did it take three of you?"

"Oh, she didn't want to go."

It always takes more work if we try to help someone who doesn't want or need assistance. We would be foolish to jump in and help our parents cross the street if they don't need our attention. It's even more foolish if they didn't even want to go in that direction to begin with.

A basic mistake many adult children make is to confuse their need to be caretakers with the real needs of their aging parents. Whose need is really being met here?

Never over-water plants.

Never over-cook sweet corn.

Never over-cut the lawn.

And never—ever—over-dote on aging parents.

Imagine for a moment that President Carter's family had wasted their time rescuing Jimmy's widowed mother, Lillian. The sixty-eight-year-old registered nurse may have missed her two-year tour of duty in India with the Peace Corps. All because her family rushed in too quickly to protect her.

When a parent keeps insisting that he or she can take care of himself, maybe that's the truth. When he says, "Don't worry about me," that may be exactly what he means. If we worry anyway, it's usually detrimental to everyone.

Don't help if you can help it.

Help only when it's really helpful.

Never help just because you can't stop helping.

I know a man age eighty-two who lives in a nursing home. Every morning at dawn the cooks carefully prepare his breakfast. They measure salt, spoon out bran flakes, and slice fruit. He gets the correct amount of juice, and naturally the nurses make sure he has his allotted number of pills.

The staff works hard to keep my friend healthy so he will live his prescribed years. They are to be commended.

Right after he finishes eating and is fully dressed, this retired farmer strolls downtown and finds a booth in the local cafe. There he orders his regular breakfast of coffee, sausage, eggs, hash browns, and toast.

Every morning this happy octogenarian eats two breakfasts. The first one he eats to please the doctors, nurses, dieticians, and other caretakers. The second breakfast he eats to meet his own needs. This double diet seems to keep him healthy as a horse. All of us should jump in and help our parents. The only problem might be that we could dive in ten or twenty years too soon.

Beware of the fifty-year-old couple who are running out of things to do. Their last child married two months ago and they are already bored. Like someone said, they are left hanging halfway between Pampers and Depends. You can see them glide over toward their parents. Isn't there something they can do for seventy-one-year-old Mom and seventy-two-year-old Dad?

The need they sense, the gap they feel, the problem they are sniffing out may not be their parent's at all. Good Chris-

tian people, they could be looking to satisfy their own empti-
ness, and they don't even realize it.

My friend Cliff cares about his mother, keeps in touch,
helps her choose a car. By any standard he is a good, dependable son who wants to help.

But Cliff is careful not to take over. If he had been doting
over her, she may not have gone to Haiti to work with children when she was eighty-one years old. If her children were
busy protecting her, she may not have gone back to war-torn
Haiti again when she was eighty-three.

Don't assume that *elderly* means fragile. Don't assume
that the elderly need to be coddled and served. Our eager-
ness to get involved can too easily conflict with their dreams,
potential, and energy.

We never had to worry that my dad would run out of
things to do. Instead of taking over for him, we let my father
take care of his own home. His job was to call the plumbers
and painters and carpenters and electricians and any other
maintenance people he might need.

Since most of the workers didn't show up when they
promised, he would call back regularly. Before long Dad
knew every receptionist, secretary, and telephone operator in
town. When the workers showed up he got to know them.
For four and a half years he stayed deeply entangled in running his own affairs and he seemed to delight in it.

There are many variables that will determine whether or
not to get involved, as well as how much help we should
offer. Each individual or family must calculate their turning
points. Later in the book we will discuss the best ways to
help. But one of our basic principles remains the same: go
slow.

Look for wisdom in the Scriptures. The Bible tells us
often that God uses the elderly. They are not regarded as
shelf items to be stored until their expiration date passes.

Consider God's attitude toward the aged. The Lord treats them as productive members of His family.

Remind yourself of these passages as you make choices.

• *Never stick Moses in the attic.*

If there had been a mandatory retirement age or government care at a set age, half of Moses' life would have been wasted. Up to the time of his death Moses was sharp. This disciple of God had good faculties and great vigor until the end.

"Moses was 120 years old when he died. Yet his eyesight was perfect and he was as strong as a young man" (Deuteronomy 34:7 TLB).

Age does not equal infirmity.

Age does not mean senility.

Age is not a synonym for dependence.

Never stick Moses in the attic.

• *Most can expect full lives.*

Never tell others when their lives are over. The workplace may let them go at a mystical age. The children might treat a widowed mother like an empty vessel. But it isn't fair to tell someone else to start winding down his or her life.

The temptation to give up is strong enough as it is. Don't contribute to geriatric delinquency by persuading elderly relatives that it's time to pack it in. They may not be Moses, but they probably have a lot of living to do.

"I will satisfy him with a full life and give him my salvation" (Psalm 91:16 TLB).

• *There is plenty of productivity left.*

Does the word *productivity* make you think of installing windshield wipers on cars at a General Motor's assembly plant? It doesn't have to. A "productive" life could consist of giving advice to young people, loving a grandchild, working the soup kitchen, painting chairs at church, or doing mission work in Appalachia.

Most elderly people could remain alert and even active until close to the time they die. It would be cruel for us to interfere and cut off their productivity. The Lord promises to use many of us late into life.

Speaking of the godly, the psalmist wrote, "For they are transplanted into the Lord's own garden, and are under his personal care. Even in old age they will still produce fruit and be vital and green. This honors the Lord, and exhibits his faithful care. He is my shelter. There is nothing but goodness in him" (Psalm 92:13–15 TLB).

In Catherine Marshall's book *To Live Again,* she discusses how important it was to find work for her hands to do. When her husband, Peter Marshall, died, she soon began to put his sermons together for a book. Mrs. Marshall needed financial support for herself and her son, but she also needed a productive life. Consequently she began to pray for ways to make money that would also "lighten the tasks or illumine the lives" of her contemporaries.

It's inspiring to watch the elderly prepare taxes for others, teach English to immigrants, help young fathers study for their GEDs, and build cabins at local camps. They are too young, too spry, too bright, too dedicated to the Lord to settle for a daybed in someone's attic.

3

TEN BIBLICAL PRINCIPLES

Times and circumstances change. What is vogue today is out of style tomorrow. Sometimes we may be bewildered by the changing situations with aging parents. It may be hard to know what to do under what conditions.

When life seems to be whirling around our heads, it is good to know that some things are dependable. Once in a while check out these ten biblical principles and make sure your feet are still planted on the ground.

1. *Show respect for parents.*

"Honor your father and your mother, so that you may live long in the land the Lord your God is giving you" (Exodus 20:12).

2. *Speak kindly to the elderly.*

"Do not rebuke an older man harshly, but exhort him as if he were your father" (1 Timothy 5:1).

3. *Look to older people for good sources of wisdom.*

"Is not wisdom found among the aged? Does not long life bring understanding?" (Job 12:12).

4. *Accept what the elderly have to offer.*

"They will still bear fruit in old age, they will stay fresh and green" (Psalm 92:14).

5. *Gratefully support your parents.*

"If anyone does not provide for his relatives, and especially for his immediate family, he has denied the faith and is worse than an unbeliever" (1 Timothy 5:8).

6. *Take pride in your parents.*

"Children's children are a crown to the aged, and parents are the pride of their children" (Proverbs 17:6).

7. *Disrespect your parents to your peril.*

"The eye that mocks a father, that scorns obedience to a mother, will be pecked out by the ravens of the valley, will be eaten by the vultures" (Proverbs 30:17).

8. *Don't rob your parents.*

"He who robs his father and drives out his mother is a son who brings shame and disgrace" (Proverbs 19:26).

9. *Don't despise your parents.*

"Listen to your father, who gave you life, and do not despise your mother when she is old" (Proverbs 23:22).

10. *Realize that your behavior affects your parents.*

"The father of a righteous man has great joy; he who has a wise son delights in him" (Proverbs 23:24).

The Bible holds children to a high and noble standard when it comes to their parents. Its guidelines provide clear goals when life starts to get fuzzy.

Unfortunately some children have suffered abuse or have been abandoned; they have serious problems applying these principles. Hopefully they will seek out a minister or other capable counselor to help them deal with these difficulties.

4

TO HONOR OUR PARENTS

Every adult child needs to grapple with this overriding moral question: What does it mean to honor one's father and mother? At first blush this part of the Ten Commandments (Exodus 20:12) seems simple and straightforward. But we are not prepared to adequately interact with our aging parents until we reach a thorough understanding of one of God's oldest laws.

Let's look at the subject, dissect the meaning, and see how we might apply it in various circumstances.

What is *honor*?

The word means to esteem, respect, value, or elevate. For an excellent synonym, look at Leviticus 19:3:

"Each of you must respect his mother and father."

Notice that compared to the command in Exodus 20:12 the order is reversed with mother mentioned first and respect replaces honor. Anyone who cursed his parents could be put to death (Leviticus 20:9) although there is no record of a child in biblical history being executed for this.

Those who show respect for their parents could live long lives (Exodus 20:12). Other situations, however, might arise and cut that person's life short. (We don't assume that anyone who dies young must have mistreated his parents.)

The New Testament confirms the Old Testament teaching

Most Old Testament laws are not reiterated in the New Testament, but this one is. In Ephesians 6:1–2 Paul tells chil-

25

dren to obey and honor their parents. He also reminds them that their lives could be long and prosperous if they keep these rules.

This spells out a wholesome, fulfilling relationship. As we grow up, ideally we both obey and show proper respect for the people who raise us to adulthood.

This is God's plan for the family. While children develop their own identity, they are forbidden to rebel. The best care and guidance most of us receive is from our parents.

We get married

Our relationship with our parents changes drastically when we get married. We leave our mother and father and cleave to our spouse. This was always God's plan for most of us. The first couple were told that marriage would work this way (Genesis 2:24). This same message is repeated throughout the Old and New Testaments (Malachi 2:15; Matthew 19:5; Ephesians 5:31).

There have always been exceptions to this, as there are today. Some adults don't get married. Others get married and don't stay married for one reason or another.

Those who do not marry and live on their own become independent. They are responsible for their living conditions and moral judgments. It would be difficult for anyone to obey another person instead of run his or her own life.

Therefore, adult children are not expected to obey their parents. Parents do not parent adult children who can function independently.

We no longer obey our parents; but do we respect them?

Some frustrated elderly parents confuse this issue. They need their adult children, and they want their help. Afraid they can't get what they need, they order their children to comply and they expect obedience. This is a big mistake born out of fear. Elderly parents must learn to ask and not to demand. Grown children are under no obligation to obey. Often they are eager to assist, but they resist being ordered around like kids. Smart parents learn to negotiate and explain what they need. Patience is a necessary virtue when dealing with adult children.

Respect runs two ways

To attain maximum respect, children must respect their parents and parents must respect adult children. Problems arise when either side demands more than it is willing to give.

The Bible teaches us that honor belongs to everyone. "Show proper respect to everyone" (1 Peter 2:17).

Each of us would be wise to spend more time doling out respect and less effort worrying about how much we receive. Our obsession with respect leaves us bent out of shape.

Not everyone deserves respect

How much honor do we give to parents who have abused, neglected, and even abandoned us? The dilemma plagues millions who have been mistreated, and yet they want to do what God teaches.

If an adult child has been sexually abused by her father, is she still obligated to show him respect? This would put many adults in a terrible spiritual and psychological bind. Let's look at two principles that shed some light.

1. *People who do good should be honored.*

Romans 2:10 says, "But [there will be] glory, honor and peace for everyone who does good: first for the Jew, then for the Gentile." Honor belongs to people who do good. Honor is not necessarily the natural right of those who do bad.

2. *Abusers are condemned.*

Jesus Christ taught that anyone who causes a child to sin would be better off if a millstone were placed around his neck and he would be dumped in the sea (Matthew 18:6).

There is no call in the Scriptures for us to pay respect to parents who have abused us. Through spiritual healing and reconciliation honor might be attainable, but it isn't automatic.

Adult children should not feel guilty if they fail to honor abusive parents. First they need to deal with the problems that have beset them; then they might be able to rise up to respect. It is possible to honor an abusive parent, but only after the situation has been resolved.

The author of Proverbs tells us that respect is something to be earned.

"A kindhearted woman gains respect, but ruthless men gain only wealth" (11:16).

God blesses good children

Those who treat their parents well can expect the blessing of God on their lives. Those who neglect and mistreat parents will fall short of God's blessing. Those are two principles that are replete throughout the Bible.

Blessing doesn't necessarily mean a prosperous business or good health. Too often we center our attention on those two commodities.

God may give peace, joy, contentment, satisfaction, and even added faith to those who honor their parents. The commandment (Exodus 20:12) promises that those who obey may live long in the land. The New Testament says that "it may go well with you" (Ephesians 6:3).

The promise isn't a good-luck charm. We don't take care of our parents so our personal portfolio will be larger. Neither do we call them once a week just to increase our sales volume. Rather we pay homage to our parents because it is right. When we do what is right, God enriches our spirits and souls with His Spirit.

Would God bless a nation whose people consistently treated their parents well? That is a distinct possibility.

On the other hand, Scripture suggests that those who neglect or degrade their parents will be deprived of God's blessing.

"If a man curses his father or mother, his lamp will be snuffed out in pitch darkness" (Proverbs 20:20).

"The eye that mocks a father, that scorns obedience to a mother, will be pecked out by the ravens of the valley, will be eaten by the vultures" (Proverbs 30:17).

If we don't know exactly how God will carry out this curse, we can be sure of this much: it doesn't sound good.

This we have learned: God puts a high priority on how we treat our parents. There may be some exceptions to these guidelines, but the principles remain the same. Under normal conditions we are expected to honor and respect our parents.

What these Scriptures say to our society

Beware of trends that worship youth. Any society that wants to shuffle off the elderly and hide them behind the scenes is messing with a group that God highly respects.

Pay attention when:

• Churches reject fifty-five-year-old pastors.
• Companies fire sixty-year-old employees.
• Mandatory retirement ages are strictly enforced.
• Receptionists over forty are removed.
• The sick are encouraged to die.
• Adult children mock their parents.
• Experience is derided.

These are not the signs of a godly or healthy society. People of all ages are needed to contribute to our total well-being. Any nation that rejects the elderly will wake up some day without wisdom or experience.

A powerful verse in Leviticus tells us to "rise in the presence of the aged, show respect for the elderly and revere your God. I am the Lord" (19:32).

Unfortunately, many have done the opposite. Instead of honoring the elderly, they have attacked and dismissed them. Isaiah discussed this same abuse in his judgment on Jerusalem.

"People will oppress each other—man against man, neighbor against neighbor. The young will rise up against the old, the base against the honorable" (3:5).

When a society neglects or degrades the elderly, those of advanced age are forced to cry out for dignity. They complain, object, and protest. The elderly demand that they be respected.

This shouldn't happen. They should receive recognition, honor and accommodations without calling attention to themselves. The Bible teaches us, "It is not good to eat too much honey, nor is it honorable to seek one's own honor" (Proverbs 25:27).

It is shameful to ignore the elderly and make them insist on appropriate respect. If the local church needs young people to give it guidance, it also needs older people to furnish wisdom.

Christ's example

While Jesus was dying on the cross for the world, He still managed to maintain a relationship with His mother. That speaks heavily to those of us who think we are too busy in our careers to keep in touch.

From the cross, Christ makes sure that someone will take care of His mother when He is gone. There are several reasons to believe that Joseph, His stepfather, had died. We aren't sure why His brothers don't take this responsibility. Maybe they would have, but Jesus isn't waiting to see. He is the oldest, and there is a special bond of faith between Him and His mother. Whatever the reasons, Christ doesn't shrink back.

He sees his mother standing next to His beloved disciple (evidently John.) Almost playfully Jesus introduces them, though they probably know each other well.

"Dear woman, here is your son . . . Here is your mother" (John 19:26–27).

From that time on, the Bible tells us, this disciple took her to live in his home. Christ's example is a great guide. We may have trouble working out details, but the principles are perfectly clear.

Many states have tried to pass filial laws, and some have them on the books. These are attempts to force family members to care for their elderly relatives. More importantly for Christians is our desire to care for and support each other in love. We need to take the Scriptures and Christ's example seriously.

Anyone who flippantly disregards his or her parents shows deep disrespect. Whenever possible, we must rise up to take a higher road and demonstrate true honor to those who cared and provided for us.

5

WHAT THEY WISH WE UNDERSTOOD

The best way to understand aging parents is to listen to them. No number of theories or guesses or books can begin to tell us as much about the elderly as the elderly themselves can tell us.

Because we often think we know what is best for children, we don't ask them. The temptation is to treat the elderly the same. But how do we know what they want unless we ask?

I recently asked a group of older people to respond to the question, "What do you wish your children understood about you?" They were eager to speak up and explain themselves. Many acted as if they seldom had an opportunity to express their feelings.

Take time to understand

"Take time to understand us, ask about our interests, what fills and fulfills our time and us," one person wrote.

These are some other answers I received.

1. *I don't need to be entertained.*

It's more fun to be together than to go running every place.

I get tired.

We need time for the two of us to be alone.

I don't like to play games.

I like to plan ahead.

I want to get together, but I don't want to intrude.

I am slowing down.
I don't mind being alone.
2. *I love my children.* (It's as if they aren't sure we know.)
   I love them like they love their children.
   All my nagging is done in love.
   We are here to support them, not to run their lives.
   We love them regardless of what they do or don't do.
   I wish they knew how much I care.
3. *I'm not dumb.*
   We have ideas when decisions must be made.
   We have opinions that count.
   I'm getting older, but I do have a mind.
   We are not as dumb as you think we are.
4. *I care spiritually.*
   I pray for you daily.
   We want you to follow the Lord.
5. *I understand the world we live in.*
   We know about the need to plan for financial security.
   We would like you to do a better job in life than we did.
   The material part of living isn't as important as personal
      relationships.
   Genuine friendship is more important than financial
      gain.
   I do care what happens to you, not just financially but
      spiritually.
6. *I don't want to be nosy.*
   I don't want to be demanding or controlling.
   We are trying to be helpful.
   We're concerned about you.
   What you perceive as meddling is really concern.
   My input in your life is for your best interest.
   I worry about your choices.
   You can raise your families as you wish, but I'm some-
      times concerned.

7. *I feel wistful.*
   When my children were young I was at times overzeal-
   ous and admonished them too much.
   I have no favorites.

Those were the major ideas they wanted to get across.
The following is a list of other things that didn't fit as neatly
into categories:
   • Don't treat me like a mother but more like a friend.
   • We grew up with more conservative ideas.
   • Understand where we're coming from.
   • I like to be on time.
   • I don't tell you everything.
   • Everything doesn't have to be perfect.
   • When I'm hungry for a certain food, I don't want a sub-
stitute.
   • I would like to be with you more but I know you have
other friends.
   • I'm concerned about your busy and stressful lives.
   • I'm concerned about your use of tobacco.
   • I'm not always right but I still run the show (in the
business).
   • I'm everybody's resource and it wears me out.
   • We've been there before and not that long ago.

What do you want

Armed with that insight, I set out to ask another question.
This time it was: "What do you want from your children?"
   • love
   • companionship
   • patience
   • respect
   • communication
   • Christian fellowship

- telephone calls
- cards and letters
- freedom to make choices
- grandchildren without the parents
- good listeners
- prayer
- availability
- visits
- money
- helpful acts
- continuing care
- honesty
- friendship
- independence
- cooperation
- acceptance
- to be included
- remember special occasions
- visits from children in other states (twice a year)
- faith in me

It would appear that the aging want pretty much the same thing the rest of us want. Nothing on the list seems totally outrageous or bizarre. Most are the common needs which are normally satisfied by good relationships.

No two aging people are likely to want the same things. The ideas may be close, but they aren't exactly alike. The best way to discover what the people in our lives need and want is to spend time asking.

The old man of the Psalms

The plight of the elderly is nothing new. Look at Psalm 31 and see a man who has stress and despair similar to the people we know. As he expresses himself, listen to his heart cry out.

Be merciful to me, O Lord, for I am in distress;
     my eyes grow weak with sorrow,
     my soul and my body with grief.
My life is consumed with anguish and my years by groaning;
     my strength fails because of my affliction,
     and my bones grow weak.
Because of all my enemies,
     I am the utter contempt of my neighbors.
I am a dread to my friends—
     those who see me on the street flee from me.
I am forgotten by them as though I were dead;
     I have become like broken pottery (9–12).

As a reality check, see how many of these words would describe your parents at this stage in their lives:

❏ distress
❏ weak eyes
❏ sorrow
❏ consumed life
❏ anguish
❏ groaning
❏ strength fails
❏ affliction
❏ weak bones
❏ enemies
❏ contempt of neighbors
❏ people flee
❏ forgotten
❏ dead
❏ broken

The psalmist uses at least seventeen expressions of personal despair. Hopefully these do not all apply to your parents. They may have seventeen expressions of joy and contentment. But the only way to be sure is to check in with them and listen.

If they are drowning in disappointment, is there something you can do to improve their lot? Maybe, and frankly, maybe not. At least we can get in touch with reality and see if it is reasonable for us to plug in.

Many of the elderly I talk to say their main needs are for friends and family—above their need for money and things. The same cry as any subculture.

"No one understands how I feel" is the woeful complaint of every age and gender in our society. Women feel like no one understands them, and men are positive that no one cares how they feel. That's the same cry uttered by every age group. Pre-schoolers, grade-schoolers, teens, young adults, middle-age parents, and the elderly all wail the same plaintive tone: "No one understands."

And each group is right. We are terribly inadequate at understanding people outside of our subculture. Few of us can comprehend why a thirteen-year-old girl wants a tattoo or why a fourteen-year-old boy would want an earring. But they do.

The only way we can cross over and begin to comprehend is by taking time to listen. We have to hear what is actually being said instead of what we think is being said.

Biblical wisdom

Scripture tells us this:

1. We can hear and not understand (Isaiah 6:9; Mark 4:12; Acts 28:26).

2. Understanding can be gained by listening attentively Proverbs 4:1).

3. Closed minds will not understand (Isaiah 44:18).

4. Fools don't have time to understand (Proverbs 18:2).

5. Patient people show great understanding (Proverbs 14:29).

There is much love between two people who take the time to understand each other.

6

THEIR HOME, YOUR HOME, OR THE NURSING HOME

When George Washington's mother, Mary, reached the age of eighty-one, she complained about her accommodations. A long-time griper, Mrs. Washington was no longer content to stay in her home at Fredricksburg. She told her son George she wanted to move.

A compassionate person, the general suggested she close up her living quarters and move in with the children. That might assuage her constant demands.

Unfortunately, George continued, there would not be room for her to stay at his Mount Vernon home. Even though the grounds encompassed a ten-miles by four-miles trek along the Potomac River, it wouldn't be nearly spacious enough for her needs. With diplomats, government officials, office seekers, old army friends and the like constantly calling on him, there would be too much commotion going on to suit her personality, he was sure of that.

While Washington could adjust his life to the rigors of war, the arrows of politicians, and the uncertainties of business, he could not bring himself to house a demanding, irritating parent. He was first in war, and first in peace, but very reluctant when it came to his dominating mother.

Fortunately, many of us have a better relationship with our parents than the father of our country had. Many get along well with their aging parents; others definitely don't. But whether we get along well or not, some decisions have to be made as our parents grow older and their abilities become more limited. Where they are going to live will become one of the paramount choices to be made. Most likely it will have to be made more than once. It's vital that everyone weigh the possibilities and discuss them. Of course the parents will make the final decision as long as they are able.

Their home

In most cases this is what the family will be dealing with. Nine out of ten elderly people remain in their own residences. Over the next decade or two that might change to eight out of ten, but the vast majority will continue this tradition.

The good news is that they will be able to remain in familiar surroundings. The bad news is that the house or apartment was built for young people and not the elderly. The worst news is that the neighborhood may have deteriorated over the past thirty years and it may no longer be safe. These are all variables that need to be factored into the equation.

If your parents remain in their house, make a checklist and be sure essential services can be maintained:

❏ Food preparation
❏ Medical attention—nurses or nursing aides
❏ House cleaning
❏ Bathing and toilet needs

They might be able to attend to all of these needs for years. If the time comes when they can't, however, other arrangements need to be pursued. We found Meals-on-Wheels a God-send for my parents. One nourishing cooked meal at noon made independent living possible. They were happy to prepare two other simple meals to supplement this healthy lunch.

Check safety features. That means rails, rails, rails. Rails in the bathroom, rails in the hall, rails on the steps. Make sure every area has adequate support.

Home accidents are one of the leading causes of death and injury among the elderly. A large number can be avoided if some simple precautions are taken. A phone-alert system may be helpful if one parent lives alone.

Walk through the house side-by-side with parents and ask the following questions:

1. How safe is this home? (stairs, throw rugs)
2. What structures may need to be changed? (wider door frames, toilet that is wheelchair accessible)
3. How practical can it be? (a lower work area in the kitchen, more telephones)
4. How secure can this place be? (door locks, fire alarms, phone next to the bed)

These needs will differ depending on the age, condition, and attitude of your parents. Try not to force a device or situation on them if they resist. Dignity is as high a priority as safety.

Ask many questions and give few commands. Most parents are not like children and should not be treated as if they are.

There are agencies who could help make a house safe for elderly. The local senior citizens' center is a good place to start the search. They not only have suggestions but might even know of someone who could help make the physical alterations. A local church might also know of retirees who would do odd jobs for a small fee or as a ministry.

No matter how many precautions we take, Christians realize that ultimate safety rests only with the Lord. After every rail is in place, every window locked, and all the wiring double-checked, our only security is found in the heavenly Father. We don't suggest this lightly. Instead of worrying about our parents, we must do what we can and leave the results in the hands of a God who loves and cares for them. That's exactly what we do in the case of our children and our spouses. So let's follow the same faith formula for our parents.

"I will lie down and sleep in peace, for you alone, O Lord, make me dwell in safety" (Psalm 4:8).

Your home

Many aging parents live with their children. Some of these families are happy as clams, while others are as restless as monkeys. There are no set rules here, but there are a few good guidelines.

"We never thought otherwise," said Norman from Atlanta. "When Grandfather died, Grandmother went to live with each of her four children. For six months we boys would double up and give her a bedroom. It didn't seem like an imposition to us. She did a lot of extra neat things for us.

"We weren't particularly happy or sad to see her come and go. It was an accepted part of life. Everyone did his part."

Despite the host of good stories available, the practice of doubling up is not as common as it once was. We asked a group of adults in their fifties how many wanted to eventually move in with one of their children. No one in the group raised a hand.

"That doesn't stop us from teasing our children about it," some said. "We keep mentioning the extra room in their house in the context of our retirement plans. Several times we have commented on how spacious their backyard is and how neatly a mobile home could be parked under the trees. We aren't serious, at least not yet, but we do teasingly want to keep their anxiety level a notch or two above the comfort level."

When our parents came to live in our town, we seriously considered living together. Why not move to a large house with separate entrances so we could share each other's company and yet enjoy privacy? Happily we decided to get a separate home for them, about six blocks away, and we never regretted the decision.

Nursing home

It isn't uncommon to meet people who love living in a nursing home. Frequently we find an elderly person who is mobile enough to live elsewhere but chooses to keep a room at the local home. If you haven't visited a nursing home for several years, it's time to become reacquainted. You will probably be pleasantly surprised. For many years I have worked and ministered in nursing homes, and I appreciate the recent improvements. Many nursing homes are changing their names to care centers, care facilities, and other designations. These new names may be an attempt to reflect new approaches and a new image. We shouldn't let prejudices cloud our thinking. If we have any concerns, we need to visit care facilities and ask questions.

It would take an entire book to cover the wide subject of nursing homes. Our role will be merely to outline a few of the important considerations to keep in mind.

Why a nursing home?

This is question number one. A nursing home isn't simply a place to "put" Mom or Dad. These facilities have specific purposes and fulfill definite roles. It would be like sending a child off to school and not asking if he or she needs an elementary school or a college.

If the goal is to find housing, or if the need is to provide medical care, the type of facility could be entirely different. Why hire doctors if Mom's need is a hot-lunch program?

Finish this sentence. "We might need to find a nursing home for Dad because . . ."

Does the rest of that sentence call for an open facility or does the parent need close attention? Age alone doesn't equal nursing home.

Ralph, at eighty-seven years, told me he wasn't ready for a nursing home. For one thing, the women were too old. For another, the worst thing wrong with him was that his knees hurt when he stood up. But most of all, he had missed his childhood and thought he would begin to enjoy his missed childhood now while he still could.

Age alone didn't make him a candidate for a retirement facility, and he didn't need long-term care.

If, however, the first question has been satisfactorily answered and a nursing home is definitely the route to go, make sure the parent is convinced. That isn't always possible, but try over a period of time to explain the situation well. Start as early to help him or her adjust to the alternatives.

Should your parent need a home, keep a few of these guidelines in mind while making the selection.

1. Is it close enough for relatives to visit?

2. Is it officially approved by a professional association and by the government?

3. Who recommends it? (The best way to find a good place is through a satisfied family.)

4. Is it clean and does it smell fresh?

5. Is the food good?

6. Is there a fair amount of activities?

7. Do groups of clergy and community groups come regularly to interact?

8. Can relatives and friends visit freely?

9. How does the staff appear to get along with each other? (This is a key to good care.)

10. Are the financial arrangements satisfactory, or is the price increasing rapidly?

11. How available are doctors and nurses?

Every family needs to complete the list for itself. What other questions are important to your particular situation? The more questions that are asked early and receive satisfactory replies, the better the relationship is likely to be. If the staff doesn't seem to have time to answer questions, this is itself a strong indication of their temperament.

When Jacob was old Joseph provided food and a place for his father to live (Genesis 47:11–12). He was glad to be in a position to help and he did what needed to be done. And when Jacob died, Joseph threw himself on his father while he wept and kissed him. God's people have a long history of caring for each other.

An in-between home

People are increasingly establishing a new station for their parents somewhere between their own homes and a nursing home. Often the elderly choose a place where they can have a large degree of independent living and a fair amount of assistance. More moderate in price than a nursing home, this option provides an array of accommodations.

Most frequently the arrangement is a private or semi-private room or apartment where parents can bring their own furniture and have room for some personal effects. Often a common dining facility is available in addition to an efficiency kitchen. For those who want companionship, a communal recreational area, a television room, or a large living room are common.

Some of the major advantages are:
- three meals
- privacy
- moderate price
- access to the outside
- companionship
- recreation

Presently these types of facilities are being built as the demand for adjustable housing increases. My wife's mother lives in an excellent facility in Maryland where these amenities and flexibility are available. It can be just the right compromise under certain circumstances. We encourage you to visit one and become acquainted with the possibilities.

Each of us has a variety of criteria to consider as we make this choice. After hearing from many families, we have devised the "Moving Questionnaire." Your circumstances may be different, but this is a place to start.

Moving Questionnaire

1. How does each person in the house get along with whoever is moving in?

2. What is the purpose of the move?

3. How long are you prepared to live together?

4. Is the person essentially a stranger?

5. Will he or she be a guest or a contributor?

6. Can you discuss house rules together?

7. Who will ultimately be in charge?

8. Is this a decision based on guilt?

9. Can any necessary alterations to the house be made?

10. Will the family now center on this person?

11. How will this change each person's lifestyle? What about ten or twenty years from now?

12. Is the person being brought in as a buffer to keep others in the house from dealing with each other?

13. How will this person add to the quality of life?

14. If necessary, will anyone be strong enough to say it is not working out?

15. How will this move affect the elderly person?

Brainstorm with the other people at your house before any decision is made. Take no one for granted. If everyone is part of the thinking process, each is far more likely to live well with the choice that is made.

Expect this decision to be stressful. Stress doesn't mean the decision is wrong. Even good things cause an increase in anxiety, so don't let that throw anyone.

Be careful of displacement. If a husband, wife, or child feels that he or she will lose value because of a new living arrangement, the move may have to wait. Everyone should understand, accept, and feel he or she is needed before any move this serious is completed.

Relocation stress

If the time comes when Mom or Dad has to move, you will need to consider the stress of relocating. When moving is handled correctly, most of the stress is manageable. But there are a few simple guidelines to keep in mind.

1. *Emphasize the positive.*

How is this move going to help? What improvements can be expected over the previous arrangement?

2. *Discuss the move well ahead of time.*

Surprises and shocks aren't helpful.

3. *Express yourself and encourage others to do the same.*

Each person should tell Grandma how eager he or she is to see the move take place.

4. *Accept negative outcome.*

Explain that the lighting may be a problem or that the sun coming through the west window in the afternoon can get uncomfortably warm. The move may not be perfect, but that's all right.

5. *Expect improvement.*

A few people become depressed after a move, but far more become exhilarated. Anticipation and a good challenge will cause many to rekindle their interest in life.

7

SIBLINGS
WORKING TOGETHER
AND DRIFTING APART

At Mother's funeral you could have cut through the tension with a knife. Three brothers and one sister with their families had returned to the mountains of Virginia out of respect for their deceased mother. Father had died eight years before; this ceremony would mark the cutting of a major rope that had tied the family together.

Because there was little money and no insurance, the children were left to pay for the funeral. Three of the adult children were content to chip in nearly a thousand dollars each. The fourth sibling asked to be excused. He was financially secure, but this brother felt it wasn't his responsibility. He had helped his mother plenty while she was alive, he reasoned; now he was determined to let the others pay the final expenses.

As the minister said the last words at the grave side, each family stood in its own group. With stern faces they turned and moved toward their vehicles. They said farewell to one another, but not to the brother who refused to pay. No one spoke to him.

This true story could be repeated in some form over and over again. Siblings, even those with the best of intentions, often fall out over the care and treatment of their parents. Frequently a good brother and a good sister are not able to agree on the best way to involve themselves in their parents' lives. Previously they had maintained close contact, but their parents' advancing years and worsening condition brought friction between them.

Like Jacob and Esau

The picture of struggling siblings isn't new to our generation. In Genesis 27 we find an aging Isaac who calls for his oldest son, Esau. The father's eyes are fading and he asks a favor of his son. He wants Esau to hunt some wild game and prepare a tasty meal. In return Isaac will give his son a special blessing.

Rebekah tells her other son, Jacob, what she had heard. Rebekah and Jacob hatch a plan to deceive dying Isaac— removing the blessing from Esau and giving it to Jacob.

Whatever the theological plan or God's will may have been, the fact is that there was a great deal of conniving going on in this family. The mother was plotting with one son against the other while the weakened elderly father couldn't trust members of his own household.

Sometimes the closest of relatives have the most outrageous battles when it comes to their own flesh and blood. At other times, simmering problems finally come to a boil after years of unresolved tension.

The fact that Father Isaac loved Esau while Mother Rebekah loved Jacob (Genesis 25:28) may have added considerably to the tension and deceit that eventually reared their heads.

Disagreements are inevitable

Very seldom are two, three, or four adult siblings going to agree on how to deal with their parents' changing circumstances. We can probably expect some discomfort and uneasiness and more than a few cases of hostility.

"I'll tell you what he does," a lady in her early fifties said about her brother. "He lives 800 miles away and bounces in here once or twice a year. That gives him three or four days a year to play the concerned son. He wants 'nothing but the best for his parents.' I've heard him say that at least a hundred times.

" 'Can't we get them out more? Shouldn't we get a doctor to look in on them? Are you sure they're eating right?' Oh, how he wishes he could be closer! 'If there is anything they need, anything at all, just let him know.'

"He jumps back in his rental car and is gone. In his mind he did what a good son is supposed to do. He stopped by, complained a lot, and took off again. 'Nothing but the best for his parents.' Then I go ahead and take care of them like I normally do."

Her story is identical to that of millions of siblings. They have a hit-and-run brother or sister who isn't able to be present, so he or she needs to make a great deal of noise to demonstrate concern. And sometimes to alleviate guilt.

"I used to resent it," she continued. "But now I understand. If he doesn't blow off a little steam, he wouldn't be able to live with himself."

Each sibling has to act or react from his or her own situation. Some are very patient and tolerant while others are short-sighted and explosive.

Jacob was also fooled

When Jacob became a father, his children grew up to deceive him in a way similar to how Jacob had fooled his father. The brothers feuded and they dumped their hated brother, Joseph, into a well (Genesis 37:22). They then smeared goat blood on Joseph's robe and took it to Father Jacob.

The brothers lied that Joseph had been killed by a ferocious animal. Jacob recognized the robe and believed his conniving sons.

Father Jacob had done much to contribute to this deceptive atmosphere. Joseph was his favorite son and the brothers knew it (Genesis 37:3). Jacob pampered the son of his old age and drew a wedge between him and the siblings.

Too often parents sow the seeds of animosity which they reap later as they grow older. When siblings have been mistreated, pitted against each other or neglected, the fires of resentment can burn inside for decades and often break into full flames when they are least expected.

Parents aren't always at fault for sibling rivalries. Sometimes brothers and sisters who got along well for years turn in opposition when their parents show signs of aging. But it certainly is important that parents deal with their children evenly and resist any temptation to stir the pot and create trouble.

Guidelines for working with siblings

When brothers and sisters are involved in helping aging parents, they are engaging in a delicate task. It would be a shame to rescue their parents and wreck the sibling relationship. And yet this is precisely what so often occurs.

Before embarking on this hazardous journey, pick up your Bible and check out these important guidelines. They are not listed in any order of importance.

1. *Weigh everyone's interests.*

Make a chart or a list and determine what everyone's needs might be. Be sure the parents' needs, the siblings' needs, and your family's needs are included. If only the parents' needs are being met, this tire will blow out sooner or later.

Read Philippians 2:4. "Each of you should look not only to your own interests, but also to the interest of others."

If decisions are made without regard to the needs, interests, and feelings of all the siblings, war will almost certainly ensue.

2. *Keep everyone informed.*

This may sound like extra work, but in the long run it is less work. It's easier to prepare than it is to repair. Read that sentence again.

Proverbs tells us, "Plans fail for a lack of counsel, but with many advisers they succeed" (15:22).

People who feel left out frequently complain about the plans. Face-to-face meetings, conference calls, and letters allow everyone to make suggestions and give input.

When my father and stepmother moved to town, I had no idea that her daughter had not been properly informed. She may have had greater peace of mind if she had been allowed to give her opinions earlier.

3. *Deal with your envy.*

If siblings have spent their lives vying for their parents' special attention, it is time to give it up. Adults have to mature and rise above envy. The issue at stake is how to help their parents. Trying to settle old scores or find new favor with aging parents is totally inappropriate.

This is no time to fight old battles. Rise above the envy and concentrate on service.

"But if you harbor bitter envy and selfish ambition in your hearts, do not boast about it or deny the truth. Such 'wisdom' does not come down from heaven but is earthly, unspiritual, of the devil" (James 3:14–15).

Questions of nursing homes, medical care, or retirement funds are not best dealt with by envious siblings. The goal is not to see who gets his or her way but rather to look for ways to help.

4. *Make peace with your siblings.*

This could be the greatest gift adult children could give to their aging parents. Brothers and sisters may have to make serious decisions with profound repercussions. Those choices are hard to make between warring factions.

None of us can afford to maintain hostilities when someone else needs help. Get together. Bury the hatchet. Find common ground. The best care and assistance will come from people who are all pulling the wagon in the same direction.

If the siblings are Christians, that is all the more reason to believe that peace is a strong possibility. Even if they aren't all believers, peace should still be a goal.

"Let the peace of Christ rule in your hearts, since as members of one body you were called to peace" (Colossians 3:15).

Christ placed a heavy emphasis on reconciliation between people. In the Sermon on the Mount He taught us, "Leave your gift there in front of the altar. First go and be reconciled to your brother; then come and offer your gift" (Matthew 5:24).

5. *Appoint someone in charge.*

Often geography and flex time will dictate which sibling should head the delegation, but make sure there is an understanding. When possible everyone will be consulted about major decisions. A designated sibling can make regular decisions when a parent can't make them.

If the brothers and sisters can agree on the formula to be followed, there will be fewer surprises and less bickering. The doctor, the lawyer, the neighbor, maybe even the plumber, should know exactly who to call. Ideally they will even know who to call if the first person on the list can't be reached.

Parents are not best served by a committee with no head. Confusion will reign supreme.

Another approach might be to make each sibling in charge of a particular area. One consults about the house and finances. Another advises about health. Know who can be counted on for which area. It's hard for someone who lives far away to be a team player, but they still could know who is responsible for what.

When Moses had more work than he could handle, his father-in-law, Jethro, told him to delegate authority. By sharing the load Moses could expect good results.

"If you do this and God so commands, you will be able to stand the strain, and all these people will go home satisfied" (Exodus 18:23).

Stand the strain and the people will go home satisfied. That's a good combination.

6. *Encourage, encourage, encourage.*

In any multiple of siblings there is likely to be at least one down-in-the-mouth, gloomy pessimist. Vow that you won't be that person.

With aging parents there is plenty to complain about. Avoid it if you can. Most days can be uplifting, rewarding, and enjoyable. There are exceptions, but life can usually be upbeat.

Don't become the complaint machine. Be realistic but hopeful. Christians shouldn't be in the habit of grinding every subject into the ground. If you can think of something good to say, say it.

For a healthy shot in the arm, read this passage frequently, "Encourage one another daily" (Hebrews 3:13).

The role shuffle

Don't assume that the sibling roles that were established in childhood will necessarily hold true as your parents age. The oldest child may have dominated the decision-making at the playground, but that might not prove true during family conferences.

The oldest child may have moved away and been out of the picture for decades. A middle child might have stayed with his or her parents, or perhaps the third child left home late and has closer contact. There is too much going on to

predict how each adult child will play out his or her part in
the unfolding drama.

The rebellious child might feel guilty.

The competitive child might need to win.

The compliant child might wax bold.

The unhealthy child might lack energy.

The child overburdened with his or her own situation
might be reluctant to get involved.

As Shakespeare told us, life is a play and it's hard to be
sure what parts we might take during each act. At times it
will be a comedy, then a mystery, then a drama, and occasionally a tragedy. Each sibling's personality, honed over the
years, may rise up to give surprising performances.

This interaction could call for an extra supply of God's
grace and an added infusion of serious prayer.

8

WHEN THERE ISN'T ENOUGH MONEY

I thank God and my father that my parents were able to bring retirement benefits with them. When they moved to our small town I was struggling to start a new career. That year brought a good increase in my income but not enough to support my parents. I remember telling myself that there was no way I would be able to purchase a better car. Not a new car. Not any car.

My parents arrived with a little money in the bank and an adequate pension plan. Whatever other wrinkles we might have to iron out, at least finances would not be a problem.

Since my dad was a federal government employee, he didn't receive regular Social Security. However, after he had been in our town for a while we realized that he might qualify. Occasionally he had worked odd jobs, had been a paid secretary for a lodge, and for years had worked Christmas holidays at a downtown Washington, D.C., department store.

We checked with the Social Security office and discovered that he did qualify for benefits.

Fortunately the great majority of elderly parents will fit into a scene similar to the one we experienced. There are many poor, elderly parents; but most are not. It is an incorrect stereotype to believe that aging and poverty are synonymous. Whenever we have met with groups to discuss aging, finances were low on the list of problems.

Ten to fourteen percent of the elderly live at the poverty level. That's sad. However, over eighty-five percent don't live at the poverty level. Therefore, it's safe to say that the average middle-age child will not be swamped with financial problems because of aging parents.

Share information

The more pressing issue for most families is how to handle the finances that are available. Since an aging person's finances could affect his or her relatives, it would be helpful if the parent shared at least an overview.

A sixty- or sixty-five-year-old parent could be expected to tell the children at least this much: "I have a small pension, Social Security, a modest investment, and the house is paid for."

Some parents will want to be specific and lay out the numbers while others won't. Privacy is important to the dignity of many, and that needs to be respected. But an adult child needs to know roughly how his parents' retirement might affect him.

One of the best ways to prime the verbal pump is for the adult child to share some information. Begin the conversation by saying, "So far this is what I've been able to start: I have an insurance policy, an annuity, and Social Security. How does that sound to you?"

With this opening the parents are less likely to become defensive. If the adult child isn't willing to share, why in the world should the parent? Never make the parent feel like an addled fool who must be treated like a child.

Once the parent is engaged in the conversation, the adult child can say, "Is that the route you're taking?" The parent has been honored because his child has shared information and valued his opinion. Parents are far more likely to open up in a friendly atmosphere instead of an interrogating atmosphere.

Round house information

For most "younger" retirees general information is all we can expect. Many are fiercely independent and don't like to give complete figures to anyone. At this stage, be happy for any information you get. If they give you numbers, that might be helpful. Or it could cause some of us to become meddlesome.

When a parent is able to manage his own finances he doesn't have to tell his children everything. Be thankful for his grit and fight.

Adult children who are available but not intrusive frequently find their parents open enough to seek them out when they sense the need. It may begin with their diminished eyesight. They will have trouble reading numbers and will ask their children to help. Information will become increasingly available as the situation changes.

Conscientious children are able to drop information. They read an article in the paper about Social Security benefits and they hand it to their parents. When the city reduces property taxes for homeowners over sixty-five, they pass on that information too. Advice will be well received if it is not demanding or belittling. Aging people welcome help if they don't sense a hook in the bait.

The direct approach

There may come a time when the adult child needs to say, "Mom, we have to talk finances." Dad may have died, an investment may have folded, bills may have gone unpaid.

At that point the parent may welcome assistance and be happy not only to reveal everything but even ask for help. If that happens, try to leave every decision possible in the hands of the parent. The rule might be: if they can, they should.

Parents may reach the stage where they need straight-talk. The talk should still be respectful and loving, but it must be honest.

What if there isn't enough?

Suppose the time has come when hard decisions must be made about finances and the money simply isn't there? How can family members act in a difficult situation?

First of all, <u>give up every recrimination</u> as soon as possible. Every day you say, "Why didn't they?" is a day of wasted energy. Blame is a drain.

Forgiveness is at the heart of creative solutions. Bitterness is the mother of destruction. We are taught to forgive others as our own transgressions are forgiven (Matthew 6:12). Wipe the slate clean and look for ways to solve the problem.

If the investment collapsed, so be it. If the retirement plan dissolved, that's unfortunate. If Mom and Dad were unwise and failed to plan ahead, that's the fact. Every accusation must be forgiven so that real progress can be made.

Second, summon the family members. Don't accept the responsibility on your shoulders alone. If a family is available, then the family must deal with the problem. The Bible lays family provision at our feet whenever possible (1 Timothy 5:8). If the siblings will cooperate, there is more wisdom because several counselors are consulted (Proverbs 15:22). Make group decisions when you can.

Third, define the need. What are the options, and how much money might be needed? Take paper and pencil.

Be realistic, frank, and honest. If some expenses are ignored or downgraded, the process is hindered. When $300 is needed, don't write down $280.

Fourth, appoint people to investigate resources. You must trust others if this is going to be a group enterprise, and indeed it should be.

Have individuals look into extra resources. Check into benefits. Are there government benefits, military, insurance, housing, or other avenues to explore?

Remind them of this truth. Every legitimate benefit they can tap into accomplishes two things. One, it helps the parent who used to help you. Two, every dollar from another source is one less dollar from the siblings' pockets. Searching for good sources is a win-win situation.

Five, kick in for the balance. Since not all siblings earn the same nor have the same resources, and since not all relatives have the same attitude, this can be ticklish. If at all feasible, every unit needs to contribute the same amount. Uneven contributions can lead to bad vibes among the siblings for decades. Look for a level playing field.

If a sibling tries to act heroic and insists on giving above his or her share, resist that offer. There may be bitter leaves or herbs at the bottom of that tea cup. However, if he or she wants to do extra, it is impractical to fight every gift or act of generosity. But where possible, agree on a base line for all.

Some families do all of this in good order and still end up with strife. None of us can ward off every conceivable contingency. Wrinkles show up in the oddest situations.

Look for solutions with great optimism. The financial need is real and the goal to correct it is a righteous one. Commit the plan to the Lord each step of the way and fully expect God to get involved.

The author of Proverbs gives us this promise: "Commit to the Lord whatever you do, and your plans will succeed" (16:3).

If you commit the project to the Lord, the finances are "do-able." The process might need to be altered from time to time. You may end up traveling down roads you didn't expect. But children with their priorities in order will find special resources from the Lord.

9

A DOZEN HINTS ON HOW TO COPE

When my parents came to live in our town we knew almost nothing about how to interact, how to help and how to cope with the situation. If we had known a few clues, we might have been more helpful to them as well as helpful to ourselves.

During those years and since we have collected some hints that other grown children might be able to use. Start with this dozen and add a few that you have learned. Anytime you feel befuddled, read these pages again to get back on track.

1. *Pull your family together.*

Don't make decisions alone. If you have an immediate family, your actions will affect them. Tell them what you are doing and why.

2. *Talk to friends.*

What do others who have assisted their parents know? Learn from their experiences and then pick and choose.

3. *Grab some literature.*

Get educated. Visit the library, check out the local bookstores, and write to organizations that work with the elderly. (See the list of resources at the end of this book.)

4. *Ask God for wisdom.*

This is an experience that will challenge you spiritually. Keep in touch with the heavenly Father.

"If any of you lacks wisdom, he should ask God, who gives generously to all without finding fault, and it will be given to him" (James 1:5).

5. *Gather resources.*

Make a list of professionals and volunteers whom you might need to draw on: doctors, nurses, social workers, senior centers, handi-buses, food suppliers, and carpenters. Most communities are packed with support people waiting to give advice and help.

6. *Cheer up your parents.*

As one becomes increasingly dependent on others, he is liable to get down on himself. Assure your parents you are in this together and the prospects are encouraging.

7. *Let parents help.*

Keep this guideline in mind: Don't do for parents what they can reasonably do for themselves.

8. *Spread the work around.*

Let grandchildren, siblings, cousins, or any other relative accept responsibilities. The work may not be divided equally, but it should be distributed.

9. *Don't fix everything.*

None of us has a perfect situation. Don't lose your mind trying to make sure your parents have everything. That easily becomes a guilt trip.

10. *Learn to say "no."*

Any individual with a life has to set boundaries. If your parents want to go someplace this weekend and you can't, then you can't. If you abandon your life for theirs, you will likely regret it.

11. *Get a grip.*

Keep close touch with a friend, a support group, or a counselor. Don't carry all the burden or swallow all the pain. If the situation begins to get to you, it helps to have someone to talk with.

12. *Plan good times.*

Lots of parties, picnics, and play times. Don't let every conversation with parents become businesslike, serious, heavy, and burdensome. Tie in plenty of laughs.

10

HOW TO HELP WIDOWS

Some of us think of widows as unfortunate old ladies who are to be pitied the rest of their lives. We know their loss is deep and emotionally crippling. We think the children will have to care for, coddle, and defend the helpless ladies for the next twenty or thirty years.

Sometimes that's true. More often the picture of the "empty" widow is totally outdated.

These days we are more likely to see widows taking college classes, bowling with the community singles group, signing up for bus tours. Go to a water exercise class at the Y and count the heads of widows bobbing along the surface. Visit senior citizens' camps and watch widows perform on skit night.

Widows don't dress in shrouds and wait out their last days in dignity. Both widows and widowers go white-water rafting.

There are record numbers of elderly in our country, and many of them live alone. Christians, both as individuals and as churches, should show compassion for people who have had such a terrible loss. Fortunately the Bible has supplied us with guidelines on how to minister to widows. Those blueprints can be just as helpful today as they were when Paul wrote them.

Instructions for widow care

The setting in which the New Testament addressed widow care was in many ways similar to our own. Most widows did not need help (except under special circumstances). When they did need it, their families were expected to take care of them. If a family was not available to meet those needs, the church would step in. However, even then the church didn't try to help everyone, but only those who qualified.

The key text is 1 Timothy 5:3–16. For easy understanding, the passage can be broken down into four sections.

The care of widows

1. Teach responsibility to their relatives, vv. 3–8
2. Help widows who qualify, vv. 9–10
3. Discourage idleness, vv. 11–15
4. Don't shift responsibility, v. 16

There has always been a need to sift out real problems from imaginary ones. The Bible displays a loving heart, not a foolish one. That's why it gives the stern warning that anyone who refuses to work should not be given any food (2 Thessalonians 3:10). Make distinctions between the truly helpless and those who merely are looking for a place to resign.

1. *Teach responsibility to their relatives,* 1 Timothy 5:3–8.

Those whose parents cared for them should eventually turn around and help those parents if the need arises. The logic is simple and direct. Adolescents may try to toss off their parents, but adults are supposed to show more maturity.

We shouldn't look for a church or any other institution to support our parents if there is any way we can. That support is certainly financial but it also may be emotional and spiritual.

Practical application: Don't call the pastor, the deacons or the benevolent fund and ask them to adopt your parents. The first line of support should come from family members.

A widow in need is a widow who has no family. The New Testament church considered such a woman as a candidate for their program. She was not automatically put into the system but she was at least evaluated. A qualified widow

(1) had no one to take care of her, and (2) could not take care of herself.

The widow who is in need should do three spiritual things (5:5):

• Put her hope in God.
• Pray day and night.
• Ask God for help.

She should not live for herself or her own pleasure (not that the widow must avoid all personal satisfaction; she can help others and still sight-see or play tennis).

Paul then repeats the major premise. Families must take care of widows if they are in want. Neglecting a parent under certain circumstances is sinful.

However, Paul in all candor does not pause to discuss the problem of abusive parents. If a parent has or continues to mistreat the child, is that child obligated to support him? There may be considerable leeway in this area. If the adult child is not strong enough to cope with maddening situations, he or she may have to look for workable alternatives.

Flat statements seldom cover every circumstance. Begin with the principle and then ask if there are other events which need to be added into the moral computer.

2. *Help widows who qualify,* 1 Timothy 5:9–10.

The church at Ephesus maintained a list of widows, and not every widow made the list.

• She had to be sixty years old. (Who can say what age that might be today?)

• She had to have a good reputation. (Good wife, servant, mother, hostess.)

• She had to devote herself to good deeds. (Not merely in the past but presently.)

Possibly the church had a group of Christian widows who dedicated themselves to serving others. In turn the church took care of these women by meeting their physical needs. They made widows part of their ministry, and the church wasn't about to incorporate non-spiritual people into a work for Christ.

3. *Discourage idleness,* 1 Timothy 5:11–15.

We all know there are problems with being labeled early in life and then spending the rest of our lives living up to that label. High-school homecoming queens can't remain that forever. The "ornery" tenth grader shouldn't become the "ornery" forty-year-old. Life changes and we have to make adjustments with it.

It must be difficult to become a widow at thirty-five. How sad it would be if her life centered on widowhood for the next fifty years. Paul says we should not assist a young woman in doing that. She needs to maintain an active life.

If the church, the community, or the family helps her concentrate on her widowhood, they do her a disservice. Many young widows remarry and successfully lead a "second life."

No one should be encouraged to "resign" from an active life too early. Most of us can be involved in a self-sufficient, meaningful, and satisfying existence even if we have suffered the horrible loss of a spouse. The person who folds up and becomes idle runs too many risks of getting into trouble and causing trouble for others.

Paul paints an unflattering picture of young widows who don't provide for themselves.

"Besides, they get into the habit of being idle and going about from house to house. And not only do they become idlers, but also gossips and busybodies, saying things they ought not to" (5:13).

4. *Don't shift responsibility,* 1 Timothy 5:16.

This is at least the third time Paul has said this. It must be important. He tells us to:

"Care for our parents" (5:4).

"Provide for our relatives" (5:8).

"Help them" (5:16).

The church should not become the main base of support for widows. Relatives should.

If we call our church and ask them to watch after our widowed parent, we may mean well. We want as much support for her or him as possible. Unfortunately we miss the point. The front line of support belongs to relatives, and Paul says bluntly, "And not let the church be burdened with them" (5:16).

Widow power

All over the country widows and widowers marshal themselves into powerful physical and spiritual forces. Their lives didn't end with the death of their spouses, and they are determined to live out their purpose.

• They organize elderly groups in their churches.

• They help people with transportation.

• They plan special weeks at camp.

• They feed people in the community with "meals on heels" for those who can walk to church.

• They take trips to mission fields where they serve as nurses, Bible teachers, sewing instructors, and carpenters.

A pivotal question for widows and widowers is whether they "disengage" from their social connections. Disengagement leaves them lonely, lethargic, and powerless. By powerless we mean they can no longer make an impact on the lives of others. They have spiritual power to help, but they lose that power when they isolate themselves.

If we live long enough, all of us will have to make this crucial decision. We may need to make it over and over again. Will we disengage ourselves from the vibrant people around us? If we do, we will probably spend our last years sitting alone on a couch, watching reruns and going to bed early. Doesn't that sound exciting?

Make the widow's heart sing

Despite Paul's emphasis on widow independence, the Scripture is constantly concerned for the widow's genuine needs. Christians are called on to aid and defend the widow who is disadvantaged and abused.

When we see a Christian shoveling the snow off a widow's walk, we know how "right" that is. Churches that have a list of "fix-it" people who are available to do simple plumbing and electrical work are citadels in defense of widows.

Maybe Job was a handyman. Can you picture him repairing cisterns and replacing roof tiles for the neighborhood widows? On the other hand he may have supplied much needed food or even offered protection against roaming criminals.

The book of Job tells us that when husbands died they blessed the name of this man of God.

"The man who was dying blessed me; I made the widow's heart sing" (Job 29:13).

In a time of terrible loss and separation, both the dying and the survivor have confidence in a person who looks out for others. This was networking at its best, long before we coined the phrase.

By looking out for widows who are "really in need" Job did the work of the Lord. One of God's major goals is to care for widows.

"He defends the cause of the fatherless and the widow, and loves the alien, giving him food and clothing" (Deuteronomy 10:18).

Helping people is a major priority for God's people. We need to do it correctly so we don't damage people in the process.

11

HOW TO GET THEM TO DO WHAT THEY DON'T WANT TO DO

Every winter ninety-three-year-old Agnes Gustafson boards an airplane in Lincoln, Nebraska, and travels to Washington state to visit her daughter and son-in-law. She changes planes in Denver. The airline officials meet her with a wheelchair and whisk her to the next flight. If there is a canceled flight which results in an overnight delay, the airline takes Mrs. Gustafson to a motel and retrieves her the next day.

How can a lady her age make this journey all alone? Two things make it possible. One, she has the confidence and drive to know she can do it. Second, her relatives stand back and let her go. They don't waste time and energy trying to stop her from being who she is.

And there's the trick. When do we stop our parents, when do we jump-start them, and when do we leave them alone? Those questions, which require the wisdom of Solomon, are ours to answer.

Leave them alone

Frequently the best answer is to leave them alone. Anyone who has tried to change someone else knows it's like forty miles of bad road. It's an unhappy prospect and the odds of accomplishing it are dismally low.

If there is any way to let someone make his own decisions, we need to let him. Repeat: If there is any way to let someone make his own decisions, we need to let him.

Take the case of Marian Hull, who lives near San Francisco. She taught school years ago and then raised her family. Afterward she believed this was the time to re-enter the labor force. Marian decided to get a part-time job to build up some Social Security.

One day she showed up for a job interview. As a friendly and loving gesture she gave the interviewer some of her homemade chocolate chip cookies.

Evidently Marian didn't take time to read any of the modern literature on how to apply for a job in this high-tech society. It's hard to imagine page 37 saying, "Be sure to bring a small plate of home-baked goodies for the interview. Milk is optional."

What would have happened if her family had gotten word of her "sweet tooth" strategy? Would they have tried to talk her out of it? Would they have suggested she take a class on applying for jobs? Would they have made her go for counseling? Fortunately everyone left her alone.

And did she get the job? Of course. The cookie-loving interviewer couldn't possibly turn Marian down.

The first rule of parent-tending is to leave them alone. Not that we don't care or visit or listen, but we don't need to intervene when things are going well.

Aging people are wise

Many societies believe the elderly are intelligent and have gained wisdom through experience. Our society has taken an unfortunate turn. Today there is a strong feeling that the elderly are slow, have diminished thinking capacities, and don't understand how life works. We feel we must therefore rescue the aging from themselves before they get hurt.

That kind of logic causes us to rush in and try to rescue anyone who is getting wrinkles. The Bible takes a different view. It treats the aging as people who are wise and who need to protect the younger generation from time to time.

The psalmist, in poetic terms, compares the righteous with palm trees and cedar trees that have been planted in the house of the Lord. Then the author makes a general observation about the righteous elderly:

> The righteous will flourish like a palm tree,
> they will grow like a cedar of Lebanon;
> planted in the house of the Lord,
> they will flourish in the courts of our God.
> They will still bear fruit in old age,
> they will stay fresh and green (92:12–14).

Many old people keep their mental and physical capabilities late in life. They stay "fresh and green." It is an enormous mistake to believe that age and senility are synonymous.

Consequently we can create one basic principle before we intervene with an elderly person: *Never make a decision for an older person if he can make that decision for himself.*

Sometimes older people pay a price for making their own decisions; but they must be afforded the right to make choices, if at all possible.

There was recently a story in the newspaper about an eighty-five-year-old man, and it does not have a happy ending. But it's an important story for those who have input into their parents' activities.

An elderly man living in the state of Oregon made his first parachute jump, but the automatic chute failed to open, and the gentleman failed to pull the cord. The man died from the fall. And while no one wanted that to happen, the man's son is reported to have said, "We'd rather see him flame out than rust out."

Old age is not a sign of confusion. Some older people are confused and others are not. Our prejudices cause us to lump everyone into a single category and proclaim all the elderly as befuddled. This is a mistake.

But what if . . .

There are times when older people need to take action but can't make the needed decision. Then, and only then, do adult children need to step in and get their parents to make choices when they don't want to.

Let's list three ways to coerce elderly persons.

• Persuade them to do what is right.
• Move them physically.
• Take legal action.

No one should resort to coercion until he is convinced that the older adult can no longer live independently. Get a marker and highlight that sentence.

Persuade them to do what is right

This is the best option of the three. It is filled with respect, love, patience, and all of the other virtues we should give to our aging parents. Some adult children don't like persuasion because they don't want to take the needed time. Time, however, is a key ingredient if we want to help others in a loving way.

The Scriptures have a great example in King David and his eighty-year-old servant, Barzillai. The king tried to persuade the old man to cross over the Jordan and live in Jerusalem (2 Samuel 19:31 ff.).

Barzillai listened to the king's offer and invitation to live in the trappings of David's splendor. But he declined. The servant said he could no longer taste good food or enjoy the sounds of good singing. The pleasure of the palace, he felt, would be wasted on him. So he didn't go.

David tried. He made his best offer. He reasoned with the eighty-year-old. But after all was said, the king allowed his servant to make his own decision. Whenever possible it's the best way to go.

"So all the people crossed the Jordan, and then the king crossed over. The king kissed Barzillai and gave him his blessing, and Barzillai returned to his home" (2 Samuel 19:39).

One of the worst things a family can do is to make plans for a relative without consulting that relative. That's the way we sometimes treat children. Perfectly sane adults with excellent reasoning abilities are moved in with family, moved to apartments, or sent to nursing homes without even being consulted. Barzillai was asked. He was made to feel welcomed. When he refused, his choice was respected. Then he was kissed and allowed to do it his way.

Too often we reason with our parents, and if they don't agree, we consider them unreasonable. It is their refusal to agree that causes us to label them as incompetent.

When we use the reasoning approach, we must accept their ability to reach a conclusion.

Taking action

There are two reasons to take action with or without the adult's consent.

1. The people they live with can no longer tolerate the circumstances.

2. The older person can no longer adequately survive in the situation.

One or both of those should be very clear. And if at all possible the adult decision-maker should discuss the circumstances with the elderly person.

"It was no longer working for us," a woman in Des Moines explained. "Mom's attitude was a big downer for everyone in our family. Meal time was depressing; the kids never seemed relaxed. My husband and I discussed little else. Right or wrong, she simply had to go."

They tried their best to describe the situation to Mom, but she wouldn't buy any of it. She had raised them and it was their turn to care for her, the way she saw it. Finally the day came; they took her and her belongings to the car and drove Mom to the care home.

This family made its decision on the basis of principle number one: The people she lived with could no longer tolerate the circumstances. Their pain threshold had been exceeded, and for the sake of all involved, a decision had to be made with or without Mom's consent. Sometimes it has to happen this way.

Fortunately, this story has a happy ending. She loves the care home. If the home has a special activity planned, she often declines to go on outings with her relatives because her new friends are so special. It was not a move she would have selected, but now she would not turn back.

If a decision has to be made without the aging person's consent, be extra sure to consult any other children and close relatives first. Unilateral decisions have a way of backfiring, especially if the elderly person resisted it in the first place.

The dignity and independence of older adults should never be trifled with. Every precaution needs to be taken to maintain their full sense of worth.

Action Checklist

Before taking action, go over a list similar to this one.

❏ Are they being adequately consulted?

❏ Are they being treated with dignity and respect?

❏ Are they being heard?

❏ Are they being given as many options as possible?

❏ Are the other relatives being used in the decision-making process?

❏ Can changes be made later?
❏ Is their age and experience being tapped?

Add other checkpoints that fit your situation. Make sure the decision is handled rationally and spiritually, as opposed to impulsively.

Reassure older parents of your continued interest

Your parents may feel as if they are being dumped. Assure them that a change in geography is not an attempt to sever the relationship. You do care and will keep contact.

Look at the last chapter of Ruth. In that great story about the love of a mother-in-law (Naomi) and a daughter-in-law (Ruth) there is a fantastic ending.

After Ruth remarried, she and Boaz were about to become parents. The ladies of the community assured Naomi that this was a good sign; Boaz would sustain Naomi in her old age (4:15) because Ruth loved her.

It's hard to beat affirmation like that. Even though circumstances change, we need to know that love does not roll away with the next wind that comes along.

Making it legal

Understandably, aging parents are reluctant to give up control to their children or any other forces. But one fact is inevitable: all of us will eventually relinquish control, even if it is by death.

The best way to settle legal matters is early, while everyone is still thinking clearly. Then review them often. Parents need to spell out what they wish to happen if they can no longer think correctly. Who will have the power to make legal and financial decisions if necessary?

Smart parents do not leave their children to hassle over the details when and if they become incapacitated. If Dad has died and Mom has Alzheimer's disease, who says where she resides and who cares for her? The children need to know who will make those decisions.

It is only fair for a grown child to ask the parent whether these legal decisions have been made. It is equally fair for the parent to explain what provisions have been made.

Get a brochure from an organization like American Association of Retired Persons or the National Institute on Aging (see index), or discuss your situation with a lawyer. Be informed and help the aging person to be informed.

What does power of attorney or executor or trustee or conservator or living will mean? More importantly, what do they mean in your state? Never rely on coffee shop wisdom.

In extreme cases there could be a conservatorship. This gives someone the power to make decisions about medicine, hospitalization, and more for an elderly person. It would be wise for the older person to have made these choices early.

Early decision-making is not morbid. Quite the contrary, it is loving and thoughtful to plan ahead and spare loved ones a great deal of agony. Explain that need to the parent involved.

Two examples

When dealing with these heavy matters, keep these two stories in mind.

1. Joseph, despite the poor way he was treated by his family, brought them to Egypt when there was terrible famine in Israel. He gathered his father, Jacob, and provided for him (Genesis 46:28–29).

2. When Father Jacob was near death he "gave these instructions" and told his family where he wanted to be buried.

"When Jacob had finished giving instructions to his sons, he drew his feet up into the bed, breathed his last and was gathered to his people" (Genesis 49:33).

After mourning his father's death, Joseph asked the Pharaoh if he could take Jacob's body and bury it. And he did.

It is best to know what our parents want, and if possible we will carry out those wishes. There may be times when we (a) don't know their wishes, (b) can't carry them out, or (c) are faced with changing circumstances. In those cases we will be forced to do the best we can, and our parents need to trust us.

Never promise a parent you will or you won't

We need to make that pledge to ourselves. Who can say what will happen ten years from now.

Don't say, "No, Mother, we will never put you in a nursing home," or "Yes, mother, we will put you in that nursing home."

Surviving children too often find themselves in an impossible bind trying to keep a promise they never should have made.

Instead say, "Yes, Mother, I know how you feel and I promise to do my best."

"My best" is a great pledge to make.

12

MARGARET WAS LONELY

Margaret is moving south. She had said she never would. Her husband, Arnold, died two years ago. She put her house on the market in November. It sold in January.

Sixty-eight years old, Margaret never thought she would leave Indiana. She and her husband had visited Florida once a year since retirement but always returned to their comfortable home in the Midwest.

This is what changed her mind.

Her husband died. Many of her friends had moved away, and others were traveling half the time. Margaret's children were kind to her and she loved her three grandchildren. But her son lived four hundred miles away and her daughter one hundred fifty.

The fact was that Margaret was lonely. Her vibrant, active friends lived in the south. She and her husband had met new friends there and Margaret had decided to join them.

This spunky, adventurous lady came to two conclusions:

1. She was lonely.
2. Loneliness was her problem to solve.

Margaret asked a neighbor to help her hook up a rental trailer to her late model LeBaron and she left.

High-risk parents

One of the most common experiences of parents is that they become lonely. People of all ages wrestle with it sometimes, but as we grow older the odds are much greater that we will sit alone, feel remorseful, and get depressed.

Change and loss are two major factors contributing to loneliness, and elderly parents often have an abundance of each. They are forced to re-create their social lives, and many don't feel up to the challenge. Most of us had trouble going to the junior high party, and we dreaded our first day at the new school. Retirees and their ilk have the same trepidation, but they are less likely to venture out into new social settings.

Widows are greatly prone toward loneliness, but so are many couples. The loss of family is a serious form of isolation for many moms and dads. Children were a major part of their social life. They met school teachers, neighbors, other parents and even an occasional truant officer through their kids. If widows fail to establish and maintain an adequate social life, the walls of loneliness begin to move in and their world starts to shrink.

Other changes such as retirement, a shrinking church, resignation from a fraternal or social club or reduced income tend to increase a person's isolation. Health problems, loss of hearing, decreased vision, limited driving, or too much worry also add to their aloneness.

It takes a brave and determined person to paddle upstream and fight the temptation to retreat to one's room, drink coffee, and watch game shows. We understand why people do it. We also know how personally destructive it is.

What should we do?

"I hate to see my parents sit home alone every night," explains Lisa. "But I can only do so much. With so many things to go to for my teenagers and my job, I can't run over there every night."

Exactly. It's hard to be responsible for someone else's social life. We might be able to help a little, but ultimately everyone must learn to deal with and resolve one's own loneliness. There are a few exceptions, such as individuals who are physically shut-in and shut down, but those situations are rare.

If we do too much for parents, we are at risk of creating what social scientists call "learned helplessness." There was a time when they could have taken care of their needs, but other people jumped in and took over. Now after years of regular assistance they have sunk into a state of helplessness.

The primary responsibility for fighting loneliness rests with the individual. It is a mistake to shift that burden and make someone else in charge of one's social life. Everyone involved could live to regret that.

Centers, barbers, and nurses

When my parents moved to our town, they left all of their friends back in Washington, D.C. In reality their social life in D.C. had reached a near standstill. Many of their friends had died and others were becoming less mobile. My parents had become quite limited as to where they could go and what they could do. Most of their friends were available only by telephone.

In their new home they missed their friends. However, more accurately, they had dreams of what they used to do with their friends. Their world had changed and could not revert to its former status.

In their new town they would have to adjust and make new choices. Would they become isolated and friendless? Would they depend solely on their family? Or would they fold up and learn to live with loneliness?

The fact is they did all three. They rejected the senior citizen's center. They didn't like the commotion, the newness, and "all those old people." Some avenues of friendship they cut off immediately.

They did however enjoy individuals in short spurts. Dale, the barber, came to cut my father's hair. Harold came from the local church to bring tapes of the services. My dad tolerated the tapes but really enjoyed Harold. The hair dresser picked up my stepmother. A nurse came regularly to check in on them and they loved her.

Others came and some took them to dinner. My father loved calling repairmen, painters, and plumbers to work on his house. He enjoyed telling them old jokes.

The rest of the time our family either visited them, took them out to eat, or went to school events so they could watch their grandchildren. We wanted to help, to be part of their lives and yet not be the sole providers of their social life. It wasn't easy and we had trouble finding the right balance.

Some decisions they had to make. How sociable did they want to be? Under what conditions did they want to get together with others?

Socially acceptable guidelines

Begin by looking to the Bible for some timeless clues. What are the principles we need to keep in mind?

1. *Encourage the elderly to keep their friends.*

Be slow to accept any arrangement which is likely to cut parents off from their friends. New friendships take work. It's easy to stop trying.

Don't be party to any situation which is prone to isolate your parents. Keep the people lines open.

"Do not forsake your friend and the friend of your father" (Proverbs 27:10).

Unnecessary separation from friends is a big mistake.

2. *Learn to rely on neighbors.*

If we prove to be good neighbors, they will probably respond by helping us. Neighbors who are ignored are hard to find when you need them.

When neighbors offer to help or get involved, don't turn them down. Good neighbors are a vital part of good networking. Don't use or abuse them, and don't reject their efforts to be friendly. Aging parents should reach out to friendly neighbors if at all possible.

"Better a neighbor nearby than a brother far away" (Proverbs 27:10).

It would be foolish to moan over the relative who isn't there and reject the neighbor who is.

3. *Connect with the church.*

Many churches provide fellowship for those past middle age.

One, they create groups whereby the elderly help one another. (The elderly get together regularly to do things and go places.)

Two, they provide volunteer work for older people. (There are opportunities to teach, paint, and go on mission trips.)

Churches are a valuable source for those who want to participate. If your local church doesn't offer such fellowship, now might be a good time to start.

The pattern is found in Acts 2:46–47. "Every day they continued to meet together in the temple courts. They broke bread in their homes and ate together with glad and sincere hearts, praising God and enjoying the favor of all the people. And the Lord added to their number daily those who were being saved."

Connecting with the church doesn't mean getting the pastor to become caretaker for our parents. Too often we ask the pastor to visit our relatives in order to fulfill our obligation. This isn't what fellowship means.

Fellowship is interaction. Adults can make meaningful connections by contributing and receiving in a helpful way.

4. *Connect with families.*

While a parent must take responsibility for his own loneliness, the child is not totally free of responsibility. A parent who spent twenty years or so caring for a child should not be cut off and cast adrift without any contact. A parent who has loved and provided for his children has hopefully established a bond which cannot be severed. True love cannot be dropped like a trash bag to be seen no more.

The author of Psalm 68:6 uses this engaging phrase, "God sets the lonely in families."

The Lord has ways of providing families for those who are isolated. In most cases that will be fellow Christians who reach out and care for each other. The writer's intention was that believers would respond and adopt anyone who needs attention.

However, those who already have families of functional people should expect a reasonable amount of company, care, and support. The body of believers should respond as well as our natural families. Both are important.

But every elderly person needs to accept responsibility for his or her own companionship if at all possible. One must reach out to his family, church, and community to dispel his own loneliness.

Particularly widows

Widows (as well as widowers) understandably report a high amount of loneliness. For years, probably decades, a woman shared her life with a companion. Her lifestyle has changed drastically. The adjustment can be difficult and she might wrestle with bouts of depression.

Fortunately there is good news. Many widows and widowers (even most), come out of their loneliness. They re-create their lives, change their routines, meet new friends, and reach out to others.

Neither increasing age nor separation from loved ones needs to result in loneliness. Those who decide to live again and accept the challenge of living manage to open up and find satisfaction.

13

THE ORPHANED PARENT

Because of our rapidly changing times and attitudes, many parents are likely to become orphans. Families, churches, and social institutions need to become aware of this growing problem.

Five social changes have created this new class of adults.

1. Parents are less likely to own family land or a business. In previous generations grandparents frequently controlled the following two or three generations through financial interests.

2. Mobility has divided family members by thousands of miles.

3. Governments have assumed more responsibility for the elderly.

4. Dysfunctional and divorced families have little interaction with each other.

5. Fewer couples are growing old together because of divorce. Traditionally marriage partners saw each other through the latter years.

Case in point

Dad is eighty-five years old, in failing health, and widowed.

Son Ron lives 1,600 miles away. Another son, David, lives across town. David is sixty-five years old, divorced, has just retired and is being treated for cancer. David's daughter, Linda, is forty-two, married, works full-time, and supports one college student and one high school senior.

With those mathematical equations, the question is, Who takes care of eighty-year-old Dad on a regular basis? One very likely answer is "none of the above." That is, Dad may be cared for by David's divorced wife (whom we didn't meet) or the United States government.

This is often the answer because:

• A woman is usually the nurturer.

• Dad paid massive sums to the government, and he's entitled to get a little of it back.

• Other relatives have become self-absorbed.

Family care is rarely the neat little package we always imagined. If we were to study one hundred families, many scenarios are possible; but the one described above is highly likely to occur.

The legal issue

Because the ramifications of moral responsibly have become so cloudy, many states have raised the question of legal responsibility. At least half of the states have toiled with the possibility of establishing laws that require families to support members who cannot support themselves. Whether such laws are actually constitutional may have to be resolved by higher courts.

With divorces and remarriages so prevalent and with so many couples having no children, the types of legal problems might be difficult to handle.

One of the more forceful legal arguments is based on the fact that parents have cared for and spent large sums of money to raise their children. This, supposedly, places an obligation on the children to reciprocate, especially in financial matters. What of parents who didn't contribute? But what of parents who only contributed for eight years? The legal hassles could be unmanageable.

Moral responsibility

Christians must first respond to higher laws than those of the country. Moral laws and biblical laws are of first concern to believers. The lack of civil law does not settle the matter for those of us who are followers of Christ.

Previously we mentioned biblical guidelines which should control our morality. Here are more principles to keep in mind.

• Christians must provide for their families (1 Timothy 5:8).

• Christians should provide for family widows (1 Timothy 5:4).

• Christians should provide for grandparents (1 Timothy 5:4).

• The church should help provide for widows who have no one to take care of them (1 Timothy 5:5).

• Jesus provided for His mother (John 19:26–27).

In Jesus' time when widows had few rights or opportunities, these principles were especially valuable. The same moral responsibilities apply today and can be exercised by every Christian who has an extended family to care for.

Another case in point

Reginald, age seventy-six, remarried two years after his wife died. His bride was seventy and they were married three years when Reginald died. His new wife, now seventy-three, recently suffered a stroke and became confined to a nursing home.

With little more than Social Security to cover the costs, the new wife had serious financial problems. Reginald's children (two daughters and a son) met to discuss the issue.

She was not their mother. They barely knew the lady. She was their father's partner, not their's. Should they walk away and let the state care for her? Or was Dad's commitment their commitment too?

How does one resolve matters of the heart?

Cheerfully, in this case, the children chose to support the widow the remainder of her life.

14

ACTIVITY IS A KEY

"Frankly, I couldn't find them home."

That's what a frustrated pastor in Minnesota said. The church he served had a long-standing tradition that the pastor call regularly on all widows in the church.

"But I couldn't find them," he went on. "Week after week I would call at a widow's house only to discover that she was at aerobics class or had gone to California to see an old friend or was on a cruise someplace. It looked to me like she was getting around a lot better than I was."

The fact that someone is elderly or widowed doesn't necessarily mean that he or she is shut-in. Some middle-age children worry about the frailty of their parents who aren't frail at all.

Recently a church committee met to consider the needs of their widows and to resolve how the church could best minister to those who have lost a spouse. They invited a widow in to discuss the subject.

"I don't need someone to minister to me," she explained. "What I need is a ministry. Tell me how I can help others. The last thing I need is a committee to watch over me."

Nearly 85 percent of the elderly in this country are considered healthy enough to remain active. "Elderly," "illness," "incapacitated," and "handicapped" are not synonymous. Most people in the sixty-five- to eighty-five-year-old group are more than capable of leading energetic, productive lives.

Activity is at the heart of health

The elderly who get out, move around, and jog their brain power are likely to stay healthy and ward off serious illness. Those who become fearful and over-dependent, allowing others to think and act on their behalf seem to acquire the most problems the earliest.

Studies indicate that those who stop walking lose their ability to walk. Often we think it's the other way around. We imagine older people don't get around because they can't. More frequently they stop getting around and soon find themselves immobile.

The same is true of mental abilities. The stereotype is that the aging lose their faculties to think well; so they reason, read and calculate less. Often the problem is that they stopped using their mental abilities and those abilities become dulled from inactivity.

Elderly people who return to school or to the work force frequently regain their brightness in a short period of time. A person who sits at home and accepts few mental challenges could suffer from a lack of interaction.

The old stereotype of the "widow's row" at church has changed drastically. The widows of our town get together for coffee, bowling, bus trips, cruises, and car tours. Some golf, teach classes at church, and work part-time.

Since this is no longer a man's world, widows feel less inhibited and feel free to enjoy the rest of their lives. Some have more discretionary income than they expected and have decided not to wilt away.

Fast food restaurants

Some restaurants make it a special point to hire people like our older parents. And often the elderly prefer to work because they enjoy a fast pace. They don't like to stand around and look busy. They like to be busy.

One restaurant chain reports a lady who began working there at the age of seventy-eight. Evidently she decided to establish a new career. Today, at ninety years of age, she is still working, and calling herself "a recycled teenager."

According to many managers, most elderly workers make coworkers and customers feel great. Little children are especially drawn to the aging and often insist on hugging an elderly worker. The presence of older workers changes the atmosphere, creating a well-rounded wholesomeness that makes families feel welcomed.

Our big concern

Many middle-age children worry unnecessarily that their parents are going to get hurt. Of course they could get hurt. Anyone could. But much of that fear is based on unwarranted assumptions.

The fact is that every parent will eventually cease to function. Someday they will sit down, lie down, or fall down and die. The shame would be for us to worry for twenty years, afraid of what might happen to our parents.

I once asked a woman how much she worried about her ninety-year-old mother.

"Almost not at all," she replied. "Mom has done well up to this point, so we kids have decided to just let her run her own life."

They bear fruit

The author of Psalm 92 saw old age as a time when the righteous were still active in serving the Lord. While the unrighteous or the self-centered might become introverted, it is possible that the godly will keep bearing fruit like a healthy tree.

"The righteous will flourish like a palm tree, they will grow like a cedar of Lebanon; planted in the house of the Lord, they will flourish in the courts of our God. They will still bear fruit in old age, they will stay fresh and green" (v. 12–14).

Bearing fruit is so much more than mere productivity. It's frightening to hear people denounce the elderly because they no longer "produce" anything for our society. There are many fruitful people who can no longer be part of the work force.

Our minds go immediately to the fruit of the Spirit described in Galatians 5:22. The elderly are capable of showing the fruit described in that passage: love, joy, peace, patience, kindness, goodness, faithfulness, gentleness, self-control.

Each and all of these attributes are valuable, and the person who shows them is a valuable person. Every life touched by this type of fruit has been enriched. All of us know elderly parents who display these strong characteristics because the Holy Spirit controls their lives.

As the Spirit-filled elderly move around, remain active, and affect lives, to that extent all of us are better off. Consider the promise Jesus Christ made to His followers concerning bearing fruit.

"I am the vine; you are the branches. If a man remains in me and I in him, he will bear much fruit; apart from me you can do nothing" (John 15:5).

When we inhibit our older parents from active involvement in the church, we cut off that much of the fruit. When we eliminate older people from the work force, we withdraw spiritual fruit from society. When we muzzle and suppress the aging relatives in our families, we deprive that portion of God's spiritual fruit.

We are far better off if we allow the elderly the opportunity to take risks and mix with the rest of the population. Activity is one of the keys to keeping the elderly young. It's also one of the keys to making our lives satisfying and complete.

Wasted gifts

With so much emphasis on early retirement, more and more people in their late fifties are no longer active. They are stacked like wood in the backyard of life.

In many cases people want to retool, not drop out all together. But because of strong feelings against the elderly, they are often unable to get back into the mainstream.

A famous insurance company in the Midwest has started a program to alleviate this trend. They hire back their retirees as temps. If they need someone for a few days or a few weeks, the company brings back a former employee. This allows the retiree to stay in touch with changes in the business. The program draws on a valuable resource—experienced and loyal employees.

Some are suspicious that older people can't keep up with the advances in technology. Much of that feeling is based on our society's prejudices against the aging. We imagine that they are sick, slow, and fading rapidly. In reality the elderly are dependable, they often have excellent attendance records and a good work ethic.

It is heartening to see a president of the United States who calls on former presidents for advice. They are a select group who have unique experiences. Since they represent both political parties and span years of recent history, their counsel is invaluable.

Good counsel is one reason grandparents are so important when a child is born. New mothers are frequently uneasy because of their lack of experience, and especially during the first few weeks, they often will welcome a grandmother's advice.

The active elderly stay "fresh and green." They also contribute extensively to those around them. When they express a desire to get involved, encourage them to do so.

15

PROTECT THEIR RESOURCES

Roger was shocked. He couldn't believe his aging father had given nearly seven thousand dollars to a religious organization during the year. His father's income was limited to retirement funds; such a large gift put the man into financial straits.

Monthly letters came to the house, many of them marked "Personal." Each began with "Dear Edgar" and ended with an inked-in signature of the organization's president. Dad had little idea of what could be done to make mass mailings look like personal correspondence.

And the phone calls! Representatives of organizations called periodically with urgent pleas. Roger wondered how long it would be before a "road rep" called on his father to discuss changing his will.

Roger's father wasn't ignorant by any means. He took good care of himself and was a Christian of great compassion. But Roger was beginning to worry if his dad was thinking a bit less sharply than he used to. But how was Roger to find that out?

The problem is real and very complicated. Parents fight hard to maintain their independence, make their own decisions, and handle their own finances. But who can determine if they start to cross the line and begin to think fuzzily?

An old situation

In New Testament times Jesus boldly accused the Pharisees of "devouring widows' houses" (Mark 12:40). Pharisees were the religious leaders of the day, and they were stealing from the elderly to collect funds to support their "ministries." Christ said such men "will be punished most severely" (Luke 20:47).

There are all kinds of ministries in today's world. Some raise money in the most open and honest of circumstances. If they knew they were taking advantage of the elderly, they might return the money immediately. Fund-raising is not in and of itself a dirty business.

On the other hand, some fund-raising organizations are blatantly misrepresentative. When elderly are in a highly vulnerable position (emotionally or monetarily), like Roger's father, they need protection against the shady and dishonest people behind such organizations.

God tells us emphatically not to steal from widows. We shouldn't steal from anyone, but widows apparently are close to the heart of God.

"Do not take advantage of a widow or an orphan. If you do and they cry out to me, I will certainly hear their cry" (Exodus 22:22–23).

Only a low-life would knowingly take money from the elderly under false pretenses. Unfortunately many people qualify for the description, and we should be alert to them.

Not just charity groups

Religious groups that swindle the elderly are the worst because they claim to serve God.

Older people tell some horror stories about purchasing cars, home construction, and land. Some of the wisest people and shrewdest dealers have turned into putty when the right salesperson pulls them into his or her confidence.

Phony organizations have called homes to collect money for all kinds of false causes, including a group that raised funds for widows of policemen. Fortunately the police exposed that scam.

One sharp widow began going to a company for personal services. Soon a salesman befriended her and kept pushing her to buy more products. She liked the attention she was getting. She enjoyed his mannerisms and charm. Before long the woman was paying thousands of dollars for things she didn't need.

Her children asked about this steady outflow of money. Naturally she didn't want them interfering.

Eventually the woman discovered how grossly inflated the services and products were. Of her own volition she cut off all contact with the person and the business.

Not everyone sees through the scheme in time.

They don't like advice

Most of us resist advice if we don't ask for it. This includes the elderly. If we try to tell our parents what to do, often they dig in and refuse to budge. Some of us have a relationship which allows our parents to come to us, but many of us don't.

There are a few ways we might try to protect our parents. If these don't help entirely, at least they could make some difference.

1. *Ask if they want help.*

"Those bills are really growing. If you ever want to talk about them, let me know."

You placed a thought in their ears. Maybe they should, maybe they could, discuss it with you. Many parents will welcome the open door.

2. *Ask them to write for information.*

Any group or business worth a nickel should be willing to send some sort of references, financial statement, or business practices record. If they don't respond in an impressive fashion, Mother or Dad might question something they didn't before.

It's best if the parents write and evaluate on their own.

3. *Write to shady organizations.*

If we see a group preying on widows, we should take the initiative and complain. Letters and calls create pressure and could result in changes.

As defenders of widows and the elderly, we may need to raise our objections. If more Christians had objected to the practices of some religious organizations, fewer people would have been hurt. A few Christians do complain, but evidently not many.

Defending widows and orphans is the work of God. Whenever we stand up for them we share some of the Lord's passion.

"A father to the fatherless, a defender of widows, is God in his holy dwelling" (Psalm 68:5).

Why they reject help

If we put ourselves in the shoes of an aging parent, we can see why they resist help from their children. In the battle to maintain our dignity, it's difficult to concede any ground before we absolutely have to.

1. *They hate to slip.*

After a certain age, you begin to fear any sign that you can't think or otherwise function as well as you used to. It would be a terrible admission to accept the fact that you can't buy a washing machine without your daughter's help. You would hate to transfer decision-making to your child. And remember, a fifty-year-old daughter is still a child to her parents.

2. *They don't trust a child.*

The elderly are not necessarily afraid of their children (though that happens). Rather they are reluctant to accept a grown child's judgment. The elderly often think the younger generation makes poor choices. They believe we owe too much money, make foolish purchases, and aren't nearly frugal enough. Few of the elderly are eager to bow to baby-boomer value systems.

3. *Inheritance problem.*

Though this might be far from a son's or daughter's mind, aging parents might begin to wonder if their children are beginning to eye the inheritance. If we tell them they shouldn't spend so much on a backyard patio, they might question our real motives. Maybe we think they are paying three times too much for the job, but too often they become suspicious of our motives.

Don't believe that your good parents would never think that of you. From time to time all of us worry about some strange things.

The delicate balance

We may all wish there was a guaranteed formula to help protect our parents, but naturally there isn't. There are too many variables and too many human factors to consider. Caring children need to:

• Be available.
• Be flexible.
• Be tough-skinned.
• Be understanding.
• Be helpful.
• Be wise.

The Lord "keeps the widow's boundaries intact" (Proverbs 15:25). As His child and as the widow's child, we must work to accomplish the same. We may not always succeed. Sometimes those we are caring for will resist our help. But we should give it a valiant try simply because we love the person and we serve the Lord.

16

TALK ABOUT FAITH

"My children act like they don't want to talk about it. I spent my life following Christ. I always took the kids to church and read them Bible stories. Now that they are grown they hardly ever mention it at all."

This great-grandmother from Indiana spoke for many people her age. Her faith had always been important, and in her later years the Lord meant more to her than ever. Yet, when her family came to visit, this subject was given short shrift. Someone might mention it in passing, but no one wanted to get involved.

When that happens a huge gap is left in the older person's life. Often he or she is bewildered as to why faith, church, commitment, worship, and Christ are seldom topics of conversation.

What is happening to Grandma?

Statistical evidence on this subject may be weak, but this is what seems to occur with many of the elderly.

• Their church attendance dips slightly but holds stronger than most age groups.

• Their personal faith tends to deepen. No longer living on the skeptical edge, many are more likely to settle in to the comfort and reassurance that God loves them.

Contrast this, for instance, with thirty-five-year-old parents who are running hectically to promote their career, provide clothing for the children, and coach Little League. Older people are more likely to be reflective, appreciative, and secure with who they are. Consequently they are prone to live at peace with the Lord.

How much of this closeness results from their pending death it is impossible to say. But we do know it is common for the elderly to be at peace with the reality of their deaths.

Not all of this is based on speculation. A few years ago surveys indicated that 75 to 80 percent of those over fifty-five attended worship services regularly. These facts are supported by the number of elderly we see in church and by the outbreak of church groups now aimed at ministering to the aging.

Some elderly are grumpy and belligerent toward God. But a large number indicate a high interest in both organized religion and in personal faith.

Why don't the children discuss it?

Each family is different, and there are many reasons why they might avoid the subject. Let's take a quick view at a few.

- The grown child's faith is cold.
- He or she doesn't go to church.
- Their church is different than grandmother's.
- Their theology is different.
- The grown child feels guilty.
- The grandchildren have abandoned the church.
- The children don't practice the same rituals at home.
- The aging parents are domineering.
- The grown children are not believers.
- They have difficulty discussing anything personal with their parents.

And the list could go on. Ultimately the reason is a lack of transparency. For some reason a parent or child or both do not care to open themselves up, especially to this subject. If they discuss it, they will have to take risks and talk on a personal level. Personal faith is a personal subject and must be met with an accepting attitude.

They still proclaim their faith

My Aunt Mildred is in her mid-eighties, and she has openly and sincerely praised the Lord all of her life. Today she is as jubilant and as excited about Christ as any time I have ever known her.

It is stimulating to hear how much the Lord continues to bless her life. How cruel it would be if anyone tried to throw cold water on her exuberant and vocal faith.

She reminds me of the psalmist, "Even when I am old and gray, do not forsake me, O God, till I declare your power to the next generation, your might to all who are to come" (71:18).

(Don't anyone tell Aunt Mildred I suggested she was old.)

Wise children become less skittish and allow their aging relatives the opportunity to express their faith. Not only is it healthy for the relative, but the testimony has a profound effect on the family.

Who would have silenced eighty-four old Anna, the prophetess who never left the temple? This widow gave testimony that God's Son had arrived (Luke 2:36–38). As we are foolish to silence children, so we are mistaken to diminish the faith of our parents.

Look at the strong declaration of faith given in Psalm 37. Who wouldn't want their parents to give voice to this statement of faith?

"I was young and now I am old, yet I have never seen the righteous forsaken or their children begging bread" (v. 25).

Parents have vibrant testimonies similar to these. They have seen God's hand move in the good times and in the bad. They have wrestled with problems of health and death and financial hardship and marital conflict and discouragement and yet their faith came through. Young people are the poorer for not having heard about God's acts of faithfulness.

Speaking to the people of Israel, God makes this promise concerning their later years:

"Even to your old age and gray hairs I am he, I am he who will sustain you. I have made you and I will carry you; I will sustain you and I will rescue you" (Isaiah 46:4).

The elderly can find great strength from the Lord and from the Scriptures. It would be a shame if we sealed their lips from expressing that spiritual confidence.

Questions worth asking

A couple of questions directed at a parent's spiritual life may be greatly appreciated. Not probing questions. Not interrogative questions. Not the kind that sound impatient or condescending. Go for questions and comments that are broad, friendly, and open-ended. Try a few samples.

• How are things going at your church?
• Are you enjoying this book?
• How's your Bible-study group?
• Remember my new job in prayer.
• You still keep your Bible next to your bed.
• The children love the books you gave them.
• We have to get here some Sunday and go to church together.

Certainly there is risk involved when we open up a spiritual dialogue. But that risk could be well worth it. First and primarily, the communication will benefit the parent who needs this spiritual outlet. Second, it ministers to the person who removes the lid.

If we aren't comfortable with all the twists this conversation might take, maybe we need a maturing process. Discomfort is not the worst of all situations. When we were children our parents were probably uneasy when we stood in public, picked our noses, lifted our dresses, or smacked the kid next to us.

Health and faith

Studies suggest that the two leading indicators of personal satisfaction among the elderly center on their health and their faith. Family and income are also important but health and faith are major contributors.

Often health and faith are closely correlated. People who trust in the Christian beliefs are able to reduce many of the ailments normally connected with anxiety. Others feel that the Lord has directly intervened and removed an illness.

Faith in Christ is the power of hope. It is the promise of help. Faith in Christ is our source for forgiveness. It is the experience that makes us members of the family of God. With so many benefits, it is no wonder that older people count their faith as one of their greatest sources of strength.

The salute that Paul gives to Timothy's mother and grandmother is highly significant.

"I have been reminded of your sincere faith, which first lived in your grandmother Lois and in your mother Eunice and, I am persuaded, now lives in you also" (2 Timothy 1:5).

Often we owe a parent or a grandparent a note of gratitude because of the faith they lived before our eyes. Now that they are older this could be an excellent time to hear them out as they continue to share their faith in Christ.

17

FACTS ABOUT AGING

Few people age 65 to 75 report being afraid of aging, but many young people are afraid to age.

Aging parents are more likely to give money to their adult children than are children to give to their parents.

Thousands of people over fifty now have the AIDS virus.

Of accidental deaths among the elderly, 50 percent are from falls.

A large part of the prison population is becoming elderly.

Older parents help young adult children more with household help than these children assist their parents.

Three times more women than men live in nursing homes.

The vast majority of elderly will never live in nursing homes.

The majority of retirees report that they want to work part-time.

On retirement, most people have one parent still living.

Presently 40 percent of retirees have no pension other than Social Security.

Half of our adult children live within a thirty-minute drive of their parents.

The first years of retirement are often blissful and can be called the "honeymoon years."

People who go to college tend to live further away from their parents.

The crimes that most frequently affect the elderly are purse snatching, fraud, theft of mailed checks, vandalism, and harassment (especially by teenagers).

Over half of the cancer detected is found in people more than sixty-five years of age.

According to the National Institute on Aging, the most frequent types of fraud against the elderly come from sales people for:
- Health insurance
- Glasses and hearing aids
- Products for miracle cures
- Charities
- Investment opportunities
- Home repair
- Door-to-door products

The population over eighty-five years of age is the fastest growing in the United States. In the next fifty years it is expected to triple to nine million people.

Half of all crimes against the elderly go unreported.

Record numbers of people over seventy are driving cars. Unfortunately the greatest increase in driver deaths is also among those who are retired.

In modern days the longest anyone has lived was a man in Japan who was documented to have been 120 years, 237 days.

Some studies indicate that muscle strength, improved mobility and reduced frailty are possible among those who exercise even if they are ninety years old.

The average life expectancy in 1900 in the United States was forty-seven. Today it is over seventy-five years.

Deaths from heart attacks have been almost cut in half since 1950.

Older people can and often do learn new skills and activities.

A study of people in their nineties found most of them in good spirits.

When a person is sixty-five years old his average life expectancy is 16.8 years.

The risk of suicide increases with age.

Deaths from strokes have decreased by 50 percent since 1970.

The skin of smokers tends to have more wrinkles than non-smokers at the same age.

Dry skin, a frequent problem among the elderly, is partly caused by loss of sweat and oil glands.

Presently 10 percent of the elderly population suffers from urinary incontinence.

Half of those past retirement age suffer from arthritis.

Two of the biggest reasons for falls among older people are poor vision and medication that causes light-headedness.

Older men tend to be married, but older women tend to be widowed.

Three-fourths of older people consider their health to be good or excellent.

Almost three-fourths of retiree-age report that they have no difficulty managing most household activities.

Most ailments suffered by older people are not caused by simple aging. They have causes that need to be treated. A pamphlet by the National Institute on Aging tells this story:

A 101-year-old man complained to his doctor about the pain in his right leg.

"Well," said the doctor, "what can you expect for a man your age?"

"But doctor," the man replied, "my left leg is 101 and it doesn't hurt a bit."

18

A SLIPPING MEMORY

When Diane's mother answered the door, she was dressed in work clothes and her hair was askew.

"Oh, this was the day we were supposed to go to shopping," she said with surprise. "Sometimes I think I'd lose my head if it weren't attached. Come on in. I'll change right away."

While Mother was getting dressed Diane sat in the living room and wondered. This wasn't the first time Mother had forgotten. Every once in a while she acted confused. Was she starting to lose ground? Maybe Mother was getting Alzheimer's. Should I make an appointment with the doctor, wondered Diane.

If you have elderly parents, you probably have been through a scene similar to Diane's. We think we see signs of Mother or Father slipping, and we ask ourselves if we should do something. How are we to approach this changing situation?

This isn't a medical book, so it can't answer questions. However, we can suggest a few guidelines that may help you reason through the situation.

Step by step ask yourself these questions:

1. *Is it normal?*

All of us can remember missing a few appointments when we were in high school. No one suggested we were senile then; they simply called us daydreamers or worse. At forty or fifty we managed to mislay a few tools or forgot to put something in the recipe. No one had us tested.

Forgetfulness is normal. Try not to create problems where they don't exist.

2. *How sedentary are they?*

The lack of physical activity could cause a person's body to become sluggish and affect the brain. More activity, walks or exercises may improve one's memory. Parents often resign themselves to the comfort of the house, apartment, or room. The familiar surroundings call for little stimulation, and their minds may shift into stagnation.

"Why would I want visitors?" a lady nearly eighty told me. "I don't have anything to talk about anyway."

She stayed in a house alone and almost never went anywhere.

3. *Is there mental stimulation?*

Retirees who go back to school or back to work often regain a great deal of their mental faculties. They start to use numbers, solve problems, gather new information, and soon garner brain power they thought was lost.

If the elderly watch television all day or merely do nothing, their minds could simply get lazy.

4. *How wide is their social network?*

When we isolate ourselves, we tend to think less. Social conversation, the exchange of ideas, a need to help each other seems to rev up our mental engines. That's why imprisonment and isolation are so painful. Both lack mental and physical exercise.

Contact with other people is important to memory enhancement.

5. *Could they have emotional problems?*

When we suffer a great loss or slide into depression, those strong, sad thoughts can work to shut down part of our thinking process. Worries and loneliness make some of us want to stop thinking. We try to turn our minds off so we won't have to deal with an unpleasant situation.

We might be treating someone for mental loss when in reality we should be discussing their grief. That grief may have begun years ago.

6. *Do they eat well?*

The problem could be this simple and direct. Poor nutrition could seriously affect an older person's ability to remember. Often the elderly don't eat well because they don't have the drive. Why go to all that trouble, they might complain.

7. *Has their medicine been checked recently?*

Possibly the dosage needs to be corrected. Ask a doctor if the medicine needs to be re-evaluated.

8. *Is this dementia?*

We used to believe that everyone suffers severe memory loss when growing older. But according to the latest information, most of us maintain our mental abilities as we age.

However, some elderly people suffer from a form of brain disease called *dementia*. With dementia changes take place causing abnormal activities of the brain cells. Not everyone with memory problems suffers from dementia, but some do. The only way to know for sure is to contact a qualified doctor.

One of the most common forms of dementia is the disease Alzheimer's. Usually the symptoms begin slowly and they steadily worsen. Only a doctor can properly diagnose this problem and treat it appropriately.

Don't assume an elderly person has Alzheimer's or attempt to deal with it without consulting a doctor. Older people could suffer from a wide range of illnesses and should not be diagnosed by amateurs.

According to the National Institute on Aging, 8 percent of the older population suffers from Alzheimer's disease and other dementias. The problem is serious and widespread but not all-encompassing of the elderly population. Never assume that an older person has it. Compare those numbers to general depression. It is estimated that 40 percent of the elderly population suffers from some form of depression. It would be easy to confuse Alzheimer's with depression and other problems at the onset if the observer is untrained.

The large number of ailments, plus the large number of supposed ailments are contributors to the high rate of suicide among the elderly. The suicide rate among those over sixty-five is twice as high as among teenagers.

Older people do suffer from serious problems, but not every sign of forgetfulness indicates a tragedy in the making. Elderly people are often disease-free and quite capable of functioning on their own. A slipping memory from time to time may be quite normal.

Compensation

We shouldn't be too quick to feel sorry for an elderly person who appears to have memory loss. For one thing they have much more to remember. Their facts, figures, events, and stories span sixty years or more. They have a lot more to call up and recount.

Older people may not be as quick as some younger ones, but speed isn't everything. The elderly frequently have far more experience and better judgment on which to draw. If it takes a little longer to recall the information, it might well be worth the wait.

Serious options

If an aging person suffers from serious lapses in memory and can no longer be left alone, there are three major options to consider. The person can be put into a nursing home (care center), they can receive professional care at home, or they can be placed in adult day care.

Adult day care is a rapidly expanding service. A few years ago there were only 300 such centers in the United

States. In the next decade the number is predicted to leap to 10,000. The centers are not restricted to people suffering from memory problems. Many with other disabilities use these daytime accommodations.

Caregivers who work or who need some relief are able to leave their parents with other elderly people for eight or ten hours a day and bring them home at night. Some people go every weekday, while others stay only two or three days a week. Low cost and flexibility make these arrangements particularly attractive for many situations.

The opportunity to socialize is an added draw for many parents. For a few days each week they meet friends, share activities and expand their otherwise restricted environment.

Old age and gray hairs

Often adult children and their spouses are called on to care for aging people who go through difficult times. When they respond and help those who really need it, they do the work of God. The Lord loves those who are advancing into the twilight of life as well as those of a younger generation who try to meet their needs. If society casts off the elderly, God does not.

Dementia is not as widespread as some think, but it is all too prevalent. Many who suffer from it can find their needs met through institutions, friends, and loving family members.

Long ago God promised to take care of the people of Israel because He loved them. Even when they became old He would continue His protection.

"Even to your old age and gray hairs I am he, I am he who will sustain you. I have made you and I will carry you; I will sustain you and I will rescue you" (Isaiah 46:4).

When our parents reach old age and gray hair, we will try to show the compassion of the Lord.

Awareness in the work place

Because of changing family responsibilities some businesses are being forced to change. Companies are beginning to make allowances for employees who care for their aging parents.

In some cases they permit employees to come to work later if they need to meet a parent's needs or take them to a day care center. Some companies are understanding when employees need to help a parent resettle, make adjustments, or have medical work done.

As people live longer and more become involved with retired parents, our society may respond favorably to tasks that must be done. The milk of human kindness is appreciated when we are called on to show compassion for our relatives.

19

IS DEPRESSION NATURAL?

Whenever Donald called his mother in Flagstaff, she sounded lifeless and down. Her attitude made Donald feel discouraged and sad. Consequently, he called his mother as seldom as he dared.

"I understand," he said, "it's not really her fault. Old people just get that way."

Despite Donald's attempts to be rational, his assumption is incorrect. Serious depression among the elderly:

- Is not natural
- Does not happen to everyone
- Can be dealt with

Of all the stereotypes that hurt older people, this is one of the most destructive. The image depicts an elderly person sitting in a room alone, listless, unmotivated, waiting for terrible news. This bleak view of aging causes many to anticipate a dull future and actually helps bring it about.

To get a realistic handle on the subject of depression among the elderly, we must divide fact from fiction.

Not inevitable

Consider two types of depression.

1. Surface depression
2. Deep depression

We get a cut in our income; a friend gets sick; it rains on the weekend. This kind of depression is natural and strikes most of us.

Surface depression visits for a day or two. If things get especially gloomy, we may feel down for a couple of weeks. Eventually a bright light shines into our lives or we decide to buck up and take charge of our own happiness.

Surface depression can happen at any age. If we are alert, we take the necessary steps to shake it off early. Even when a loved one dies, we get a grip and get back to living no matter how much it hurts.

Deep depression is another matter. Someone goes into the dumps and stays there. Nothing seems to bring him out. His depression lasts for a month or longer. This person usually needs extra help or professional attention to pull him out of the pit.

Some of us recognize when depression sweeps over us. We might even be able to identify whether it is surface or deep. But sometimes we are no longer capable of grabbing depression by the horns and turning it around.

What's natural?

"Natural" does not mean that every elderly person eventually sinks into deep depression because it goes with old age. Many elderly people never dive into the depths of despair. They accept life as a series of ups and downs and deal with it accordingly.

Unfortunately, though, a large number of retirees do become deeply depressed. Suicides are more prevalent among the elderly than even among teenagers.

The mistake would be to accept deep depression as a normal part of aging and believe nothing can be done about it. Deep depression is not inevitable; a great deal can be done about it.

They didn't want to go on

A quick look at the Bible comes up with several godly people who didn't see any point to living.

• Elijah defeated the prophets at Mount Carmel and then told God he wanted to die (1 Kings 19:4).

• Jonah got bent out of shape over Nineveh and told God it was better if he died (Jonah 4:3).

• Job's wife got tired of seeing her husband suffer and told him to curse God and die (Job 2:9).

• The psalmist was afraid God would hide His face and leave him brokenhearted (Psalm 69:16–18).

Depression has always been a frequent visitor, even to those who have led righteous lives. We should expect to battle depression, and we should also expect to win.

How does depression affect parents?

People come in all varieties, and depression does too. Short-term, long-term, and medium. We get blue because of disappointments, isolation, self-pity, inactivity, and serious clinical problems. Often depression will come as a result of several factors merging, like three or four rivers converging to form a giant flood.

If a parent goes into a funk, we might begin by asking several questions.

1. *What has changed?*

Has someone gotten ill, died or moved away? Has there been a traumatic change in a relationship?

Is there a change in medication? Some medicines will alter a person's appetite, energy level, or zeal. Let the doctor know if depression accompanies any medical decisions.

Look for a change in eating habits. Are they cooking less, eating differently or dieting? Radical alterations in food intake often affects mood.

Is there a change in location? Have they moved from one residence to another? Elderly people frequently become sad after moving, but it usually doesn't last long. While nostalgic at first, their melancholy soon turns to acceptance and even excitement. If they don't adjust to the new surroundings, however, this could present a problem.

2. *What is the medical situation?*

Don't play doctor, but do play detective. Is it possible that the elderly person has received painful news from the physician and has failed to tell you? Ask your parents directly if they have been given depressing information from the clinic. If you aren't satisfied with their reply, call the doctor. Even if the professionals don't give you a complete answer, they should be able to drop a few hints.

3. *Any unknown illnesses?*

Suggest a physical examination simply to rule out this possibility. Some illnesses and diseases may lead to depression without the victim's knowledge. Strokes, hormonal disruptions, and Parkinson's disease can affect body chemistry before the person realizes there is a problem.

Plus, a talk with a trusted doctor might allow an elderly person the freedom to discuss whatever is going on. A trip to the doctor could benefit a depressed older person in many ways.

4. *Are there genetic difficulties?*

Is there a history of depression in the person's family? Medicine does not fully understand genetic influence, though great strides are being made. If depression runs through the family tree, a doctor should be aware of this and be given the opportunity to respond accordingly.

Most cases are treatable

The good news is that depression is highly treatable. Ministers, friends, therapists, and modern drugs have all been extremely effective when a particular problem is matched with the appropriate assistance. The vast majority of depressed people never need to enter a hospital to find a solution for depression.

It is a waste to watch elderly people drown in depression when the solution might be simple and short term. Even if the remedy is complicated, it is a shame to leave the condition untreated.

Accept our own limitations

For most people, depression is their problem and ultimately theirs alone. Others can help. Friends can make suggestions. Family can provide a bit of bait. But a person who doesn't want to rise above depression is terribly difficult to pry loose from it.

Don't say, "My father is depressed because I am unable to rescue him." That's a guilt trip and an unfair accusation against yourself. Rather, say, "My father is depressed and I am going to see if I can help." The depression itself is not your fault.

This may be rare, but it does happen. Some people use their depression as a rope to tie others up. They don't want to conquer their depression because they are afraid they will lose the attention of those caring for them.

Help someone suffering from depression, but do not assume responsibility.

What changed Elijah?

We may be able to "perk up" depressed parents if the situation is surface and temporary. Our hands are not totally tied. Continuous, warm and friendly contact can supply an emotional booster shot that helps a parent not only float but even sail.

Look carefully at the text of 1 Kings 19:3–9. This passage wasn't written to teach us how to handle depression, but it gives us an outstanding example.

Elijah's depression was surface and situational. It wasn't clinical or genetic. He had recently been on a tremendous high when he defeated Baal's prophets at Mount Carmel. From there he plummeted into the sea of despair.

Elijah hit the bottom. He prayed to die.

Three simple but profound things brought the prophet out of his depression.

1. He took a nap.
2. He got something to eat.
3. An angel touched him.

In this case the solution was physical and spiritual. He came out of his condition immediately and traveled for the next forty days and nights (v. 8).

Sometimes our depressed parents (like the rest of us) need a nap, a sandwich, and some encouragement from the Lord. Our parents might benefit from:

- a phone call
- a short note
- a few flowers
- going out for lunch
- an afternoon drive
- a short visit
- something from the grandchildren
- news that you will visit next month

If small remembrances don't work and you have exhausted all other avenues you know to try, ask about seeking professional help.

Things not to do

On rare occasions the most unusual gimmicks may pull people out of the pits. You hear bizarre stories of how people frightened their relatives or threatened them and they snapped out of it. Those illustrations are probably true, but they may backfire as often as they work.

From someone who has suffered from depression, my suggestions are:

1. *Don't demand they snap out of it.*

An impatient friend or relative will shout, "Why don't you grow up and quit feeling sorry for yourself?"

This approach may be great at creating a crisis, but it's hard to predict which way the crisis will bounce. It is a sign of frustration and is risky to the extreme.

2. *Don't say, "I'll do anything to help you."*

You set a trap for yourself, and the depressed individual might choose to use it. Be specific about what you offer to do, and don't leave it totally open-ended.

3. *Don't say, "Well, I'm leaving, call me when you decide to get over this."*

That sounds like a fair-weather friend. Tell them you will be in contact again soon. They need reassurance that they have someone to turn to when they look for a harbor.

Depression by its very nature isn't pleasant for the person or the people around. It isn't always fun to be around older people, but they didn't always enjoy being around us when we were children and teenagers.

When our parents suffer from depression (and they don't usually), they can benefit from a loving, grown child who remains steady while they are in turmoil.

Many of our parents walked the floor, holding us, while we cried all night. More than once most parents stayed up half the night wondering where their teenager was. If in turn, we spend a few evenings worrying about our elderly parents, somehow that doesn't seem unfair.

20

TOP TEN WAYS
TO BUILD UP A PARENT

Most of us happily spend time and effort to build up our friends, companions, coworkers, neighbors and fellow parishioners. The concept is good, but we can easily forget to do the same for our own parents.

We are used to thinking of our parents as self-sufficient and strong people. That may be the case, but they still need encouragement.

Almost any parent would love to hear a few of the following supportive statements:

1. I love you.
2. Thanks for all you did for me. (Be specific.)
3. It's great knowing I have you to talk with.
4. The grandchildren talk about you all of the time.
5. I want to get your opinion before I start this.
6. Would you help me with this the next time you come over?
7. I really appreciate your cheerfulness and optimism.
8. You know what my favorite trip with you was?
9. I always feel better after I visit with you.
10. Why don't you come spend the weekend with us?

Those ten are sure winners. For extra measure add these five:

1. Tell me what you have been doing today.
2. Can I help you with something while I'm here?
3. Thanks for sharing your faith with me.

4. I can see how much I look like you; I'm glad for that.

5. I'll call you the first part of next week.

None of these encouragements cost money. Some take a little time. All of them call for a bit of thoughtfulness. Careful children can help infuse energy and hope into an elderly parent.

"Reckless words pierce like a sword, but the tongue of the wise brings healing" (Proverbs 12:18).

21

TOP TEN WAYS
TO INSULT A PARENT

All of us are thoughtless sometimes. We get tired, we are in a hurry, we're frustrated. Unfortunately, thoughtlessness is a common experience, but we are reminded that love is kind (1 Corinthians 13:4).

Everyone is different, so the following are not guaranteed to insult every parent. But they are very likely to lay one's spirit low.

1. You just don't understand.

This implies they have little feeling or intelligence.

2. I don't have time to explain it.

This says they aren't worth the time.

3. Mom, you can't remember anything.

Who remembers everything?

4. Dad, nobody wants to hear those old stories.

Are today's stories the only good ones?

5. We have decided . . .

You value neither their opinion nor their autonomy.

6. Why don't you get rid of some of this junk?

Doesn't some of your "junk" hold memories as well as feelings of security?

7. We just don't have time to call.

They aren't a priority.

8. No one believes that anymore.

As if their faith and values are useless.

9. Old, sick people live too long.

They are inconvenient to have around.

10. You're the reason I have problems.

They also might be the reason you have strengths.

Bright and caring people know when to speak, and they also know how to speak kindly.

"A man of knowledge uses words with restraint, and a man of understanding is even-tempered.

"Even a fool is thought wise if he keeps silent, and discerning if he holds his tongue" (Proverbs 17:27–28).

Sometimes caregivers are wisest when they hold their tongues.

22

LOVING AND HATING
OUR PARENTS

The American Revolution nearly failed twenty years before it began. George Washington, anxious to become a combat officer, was invited to serve under General Braddock in the French and Indian War. When the young officer's mother heard of the commission, she went directly to confront him.

She informed George that as a son he had definite duties to care for his mother. His family obligations, she said, would prevent him from engaging in any type of combat.

A sad but wiser son, George Washington declined the opportunity to see battle and served instead as a supply officer on the home front. Later, however, he did join in combat and become a national hero to our fledgling country.

We can only guess how history might have changed if Washington's mother had persisted in wielding her maternal power.

The question of how much power parents should be able to sway over their grown children has always been a sensitive issue. If an aging parent says we cannot move to Seattle, should that end our dreams of the Puget Sound with seals skipping across the water? If a parent insists on living with us instead of going to a nursing home, are we bound to their demands?

Principles and guidelines

The Bible doesn't contain the words *hospital bed* or *sun room*. Neither can we expect to see instructions written on our mirror one morning after we take a shower. That's not the way it works. However, the Scriptures do give us guidelines that are helpful in decision-making, especially as they affect our aging parents.

Principle #1

Following Christ is extremely important.

One of the most difficult things Jesus told us is found in Luke 14:26.

"If anyone comes to me and does not hate his father and mother, his wife and children, his brothers and sisters—yes, even his own life—he cannot be my disciple."

Washington's obligations to his country may have been greater than his responsibilities to his mother. We aren't able to answer that with certainty, but it's possible. Parents are a very important duty but they may not be the most important. That is what Jesus implies in Luke 14:26.

This passage confuses many Christians: Is Christ really urging us to hate our parents? He isn't teaching us to hate our spouse, our children, our siblings, or our own bodies. Too many scriptures teach us to love all three.

In Luke 14:26 the word *hate* is a comparison. Jesus asks that our love for Him and our desire to follow God make our love for family look like hate by comparison.

Christians are taught to follow Christ and care for their parents as best they can. The two don't have to be mutually exclusive. We can serve the Lord in the slums of Chicago and provide for parents at the same time.

Principle #2

Don't look for ways out of your responsibility.

The hard-hearted Pharisees were guilty of using their religion to avoid caring for needy parents. Jesus accused them of ignoring their parents and simply claiming "Corban." The term *Corban* meant they gave money to the temple as an offering and expected the temple to care for their parents through some sort of benevolent fund.

"But you say that if a man says to his father or mother: 'Whatever help you might otherwise have received from me is Corban' (that is, a gift devoted to God), then you no longer let him do anything for his father or mother" (Mark 7:11–12).

The balance between "hating" our parents to serve Christ and claiming "Corban" to avoid helping them is what most Christians should seek. We can't protest that we are too pious to care for our parents. If need be, we are to leave for India as disciples for Christ and at the same time make provisions for our parents.

In an imperfect world we can't do everything as well as we might like, but we can follow a couple of markers. Some people that Christ heavily criticized had parents who could care for themselves, but these adult children instead of serving Christ now, wanted to wait around in case the parent happened to die. According to Jesus, such people have their priorities out of order.

"He said to another man, 'Follow me.'

"But the man replied, 'Lord, first let me go and bury my father.'

"Jesus said to him, 'Let the dead bury their own dead, but you go and proclaim the kingdom of God' " (Luke 9:59–60).

We glean guidelines and not laws. Who are we to say how someone else must interact with his or her aging parent? Don't let us become legalists who split hairs and look for special clauses or extenuating circumstances to furnish excuses for our behavior. These two guidelines remain paramount.

1. Love the Lord God.
2. Help our parents as they need us.

Anything we do to reconcile these two principles must lead us very close to the truth.

Principle #3

Leave your parental family for your marriage family.

There are two types of adult children: those who marry and those who remain single. Within each of those categories there are many subdivisions—those who divorce, who remarry, who are separated, who are widowed, or who live with a partner without marrying. Life isn't simple and never has been.

The Bible tells us how the parent-child relationship changes when an adult child marries. It doesn't specifically say how adult single children are to relate to their parents. There are several historical reasons for this:

Most people married.

Those who didn't marry usually lived at home or remained within the family clan.

The most prevalent question was (and still is), What is the relationship between a married adult child and his parents? With crystal clarity the answer returns: The adult child is to leave his parents and cleave to his partner (Genesis 2:24; Matthew 19:5; Ephesians 5:31).

That dual act of leaving and cleaving (or uniting) helps define our love-hate relationship with our parents.

• We may be devoted to them, but our greatest devotion is to Jesus Christ.

• We may love them, but we have a greater priority—our family.

• We try to help our parents but any help (financial, physical, spiritual) must keep our first two priorities in mind.

Ideally all three of these areas will get their proper attention. In the natural and spiritual order the first two should receive our primary attention. That's what the Bible teaches us, yet it never teaches us to neglect our parents.

The same principles apply to single adult children as far as they go. Our first obligation is to Jesus Christ and a major obligation goes to our parents. At the same time it is necessary to meet our own basic needs.

Broad strokes

None of us should get lost in the legalism of these points. This isn't a contract with dozens of *therefores* and *henceforths*. Don't get lost in the clauses. Don't stumble over the loopholes.

Love the Lord.

Care for your family.

Watch out for your parents.

Do these three things and you can be sure you are following God's design for caregiving.

23

THINGS YOU HATE TO HEAR

Some of us stay away from our aging parents because they say hurtful things. We are not fond of pain, so we aren't easily drawn to someone who is likely to hurt us.

Whenever Linda stops by to see her father, she knows which way the conversation will eventually go. They talk about the weather, their relatives in Oregon, a little baseball, and how lousy the government is run. If anything new has happened in her life, she tries to bring that up too.

But the entire time Linda is with her dad she is fidgety and uncomfortable. She's waiting for a certain sentence that will send her blood pressure up. The words sound something like: "Still carrying a little extra weight, I see."

This may be his way of showing that he still cares. It's hard to tell if he means well or if he has some other motive. He cuts deeply and Linda is never quite sure why he makes the incision.

However, she knows this much: the effect is devastating. Linda literally hates to go see her dad. She feels that whatever good the visit accomplishes is more than ruined by the wound he reopens.

Many suffer from painful jabs inflicted when they visit parents. I've asked middle-age children what they hate to hear their parents say, and a few common threads recur throughout their examples.

Painful sayings are almost always:
• deeply personal
• disappointing

- repeated frequently
- negative
- rooted in the past

There are exceptions. Some of us get tired of the same compliment visit after visit, especially if we think it is flattery and not sincerely meant. The third decade of "Why, it's my cute little girl" can be cruel no matter what the intentions.

Other things we hate to hear

The list may be long, but these few will make the point. What grinds one grown child will not necessarily bother the next. Much depends on the history behind the statement. Look at a few examples:

1. *"This generation has gone to pot."*

It's fine for them to take pride in their era, but statements like this put other generations down. No one wants to be told that he and his friends are dumb and useless. Children don't like it and neither do grandchildren.

The Depression, the War, the Sixties—all had their good points, but so did the '70s, '80s and '90s.

2. *"So you finally found time to drop by."*

This is a call for attention, but normally it has the opposite effect. The statement drips with criticism. Instead of saying they are happy to see the child, the parents stick a dagger in his heart.

It's a no-win situation. If you don't visit or call, you get blasted. If you do visit or call you get blasted. This is not a relationship-building commitment.

3. *"I didn't raise you that way."*

Parents who say this set themselves up for disaster. Often we want to scream back, "You didn't raise me at all," especially if the parent was delinquent.

The statement is an odd mixture of a play to be cute and a blunt reminder that they are still the parents. It is so packed with emotional explosives that aging parents are almost reckless if they use it.

4. *"I raised you; now it's your turn to help me."*

Tone is a big factor in this one. There is a gem of truth in this old saw, but it can easily be hurtful. Is the parent submitting a bill, making a demand, or simply kidding? Try not to take it too seriously and simply look beyond the awkward statement.

5. *"Working women are a big part of the problem."*

Some parents are insensitive to their children's feelings. They act as if age gives them a license to blurt out anything they want. Their free-wielding stabs are extremely damaging.

Not all of these tasteless comments can be attributed to senility or Alzheimer's. Some elderly merely become cranky, and they think they have a right to be disagreeable.

6. *"I don't know why I'm here anymore."*

Parents probably make depressing, defeating, and hopeless remarks for several reasons. One is because they mean them. Another is because they are crying for help. A third might be because they are trying to manipulate their children.

Many adult children hate to call or visit because they know their parents will throw buckets of cold water on their lives. A child will become confused, depressed, and upset when a mother or father paints an ugly sky on the picture of life.

Maybe your parents don't make comments you hate to hear, but many do. Their statements may differ a little, but they carry the same sting. Not every destructive remark should be ignored or accepted. For everyone's best interest, the adult child might have to take action.

How to handle hated statements

When Larry told his father to stop being so negative, it was difficult to say. Larry wasn't in the habit of correcting his dad, but he didn't have much choice. If his father continued to be so critical, Larry would visit less and less.

Mary told her mother not to mention the old boyfriend again. "Let's just drop the subject and talk about my life now," she said.

In the interest of peace and harmony, in the hope of a brighter future together, adult children may have to correct their aging parents. When done properly, that confrontation might create a better relationship. If ignored, the hated statements will probably continue to sour the connection.

The Scriptures offer some wisdom that will better enable us to handle such verbal assaults.

1. *Smart parents will listen.*

If someone tells a parent, "I don't like to be reminded about my weight," most parents will stop saying it. Should they forget and mention it again, just say, "Remember, not the weight."

That's all most parents need because they are both intelligent and wise. We all make mistakes and need to be corrected occasionally.

Part of the difficulty of doing this is that we don't like to correct our parents. But if we don't, our relationship suffers from silence. It is important to voice our feelings.

The author of Proverbs tells us the direct approach will work with people who are discerning: "A rebuke impresses a man of discernment more than a hundred lashes a fool" (17:10).

Many parents mean well and don't realize they are being offensive. Most want to become wiser and avoid hurting the people they love.

Instruct a wise man and he will be wiser still;
teach a righteous man and he will add to his learning.

(Proverbs 9:9)

2. *Don't be harsh in your correction.*

Too often we picture an adult child at his wit's end, frustrated and yelling at his aging parent. Act early to avoid such an explosion. The sooner we address a problem, the easier we can deal with it. Today is usually the best time to handle an awkward situation.

Paul is very sensitive about the way we correct the aging.

"Do not rebuke an older man harshly, but exhort him as if he were your father. Treat younger men as brothers, older women as mothers, and younger women as sisters, with absolute purity" (1 Timothy 5:1–2).

The normal, acceptable, loving way to discuss problems with aging relatives is without harshness. Adult children who threaten, verbally abuse, and even hit their elderly parents could not be farther away form biblical teaching. Though the demands of life are often painful, nothing justifies mean and cruel treatment of our parents.

3. *Confrontation can save the relationship.*

Silence mixed with bitterness will poison a parent-child relationship, no matter what ages are involved. If the child is fifteen or fifty-five, silence mixed with bitterness is cancerous.

Intelligent correction is relationship CPR. It will breathe life into dying relationships. When we see our closeness dying because of what is being said, we would be fools not to speak up.

Years ago a stepmother made a thoughtless comment to her twenty-year-old stepson. The words cut him to the core. He never told her how much it hurt, and he seldom has spoken to her for fifteen years for fear she will say it again. If he had told her how he felt, his correction could have breathed life into their relationship. Instead, he remains silent and bitter, and his stepmother is none the wiser.

"He who listens to a life-giving rebuke will be at home among the wise" (Proverbs 15:31).

4. *The principle of correction is sound.*

"It is better to heed a wise man's rebuke than to listen to the song of fools" (Ecclesiastes 7:5). Whether it applies to our parents or to ourselves, the basic principle makes sense: Let good people correct in good ways. If we learn this principle while we are relatively young, its wisdom could serve us well when we are elderly.

There is great value in direct but caring correction given for the purpose of protecting a loving relationship. We do no one service by saying everything is fine when we are raging inside.

If we hate to hear hateful comments from our parents, we need to do everyone a favor and address the problem.

24

IT IS WORTH IT

One pleasant sunny afternoon I went for a walk. With no destination in mind I walked out to the highway and soon headed north. There isn't much traffic where we live, so it's easy to walk along the roadside.

A quarter of a mile soon turned into a full mile, and I eventually found myself standing at the entrance of the county cemetery. "Why not?" I thought. I went in to stroll among the headstones.

Without a conscious decision, I came to a stop next to my father's and stepmother's graves. I read the stone and my dad's birth date jumped out at me. March 12. Today was March 12, and I hadn't even stopped to think about it. By some compulsion unknown to me I was standing at my father's grave on his birthday.

A lump came to my throat and my eyes moistened. In that moment I told him, "Thanks." Thanks for coming our way for a few years. Thanks for getting to know the grandchildren for a while.

Though we had never been close, I was still grateful to God for the few years with my dad. He added a dimension to my life that I'll always be grateful for.

I was more fortunate than my wife, whose father died when he was only fifty-three. Often I think about how much we and the children missed because he died thirty years ago.

God has blessed us with the elderly. The world would be poorer if all grandparents passed away at fifty. Their experience, their connection and their faith are too valuable to lose. So are their companionship and love.

Take another look at the story of Rahab in the book of Joshua. She may have been a prostitute (2:1), but she cared for the needs of her parents.

"Give me a sign that you will spare the lives of my father and mother, my brothers and sisters, and all who belong to them, and that you will save us from death" (2:12–13).

Rahab agreed not to expose the spies of Israel, but in return she insisted on protection for her parents and the rest of her family. The heroine at Jericho provided for those who had nurtured and loved her.

Unlike Rahab, most of us have little to do with political intrigue. But in less dramatic ways we can aid and protect our aging parents. Be encouraged.

In the peaks and valleys, crevices and contours of the snow-capped mountain adventure of caring for the aging, God will reward us, as He did Rahab, with an unexpected grace and treasure in our midst.

SOURCES OF INFORMATION

There are many good places that offer information on aging. The following are a few we found especially valuable:

National Institute on Aging
Information Center
P. O. Box 8057
Gaithersburg, MD 20898–8057

American Association of Retired Persons
601 E Street, NW
Washington, D.C. 20049

Children of Aging Parents
Woodbourne Office Campus
Suite 302A
1609 Woodbourne Road
Levittown, PA 19057

Other Discovery House books
by WILLIAM L. COLEMAN

Before the Ring—Questions Worth Asking

From Full House to Empty Nest—Learning To Enjoy Life
Again Now That Your Children Are Grown

Note to the Reader

The publisher invites you to share your response to the message of this book by writing Discovery House Publishers, P.O. Box 3566, Grand Rapids, MI 49501, U.S.A. or by calling 1-800-653-8333. For information about other Discovery House publications, contact us at the same address and phone number.